"THIS WEEK IN BLACK HISTORY"

(A Daily Journal)

FROM KINGS TO PRESIDENTS

Revised
IV
Edition

By
Willie A. Price

Published by Willie A. Price Speaks
Edited by: Willie A. Price, Monwell Floyd and Summer l. Chapman
Covers Photos by Willie A. Price and Monwell Floyd
Cover by Willie A. Price and Monwell Floyd
Original Printing by Image Printer

All rights are reserved. No part of this book may be reproduced or transmitted in any form or by means, electronic or mechanical, including photocopying or recording or by any information storage or retrieval system, without permission in writing from the publisher or author.

Printed in the United States of America

"WillieAPriceSpeaks"
P. O. Box 603, Buffalo, NY 14215
E-Mail: WillieAPrice@aol.com
Web: www.WillieAPriceSpeaks.com

Copyright © Willie A. Price 2008
Copyright©Revised2013
Price, Willie Anthony
This Week in Black History 2013, Revised Edition
From Kings To Presidents
Includes index.
ISBN-13: 978-0-9791736-3-9
ISBN-10: 0-9791736-3-9

Acknowledgment

First, I'd like to give thanks to my Lord and Savior, Who I strive daily to make the head of my life. **Philippians 4:13**

I would like to thank Mr. Maloyd Ben Wilson of the Black Chronicle Magazine, who showed me what it took to make this book a success.

To all of my teachers from Build Academy Elementary School, when it was located on Clinton St. from 1968 until 1974, for all of the spoken and unspoken lessons, which have instilled in me the appreciation of my Black heritage.

To Alnisa Banks and the staff at the Challenger Newspaper (Buffalo, N.Y.) for printing so many of my articles and giving me the motivation to put it all together.

To my very special friends Miss Sharon Quinn, Mr. Greg Williams and Mr. Les Brown, thanks for your "Special Friendships" and for your encouragement.

Thank you to Mr. Orlando Brown, Stewart Aberte, Sandy Beach, Judge Henry Nowak, Mr. Charles Fields and Ms. Paula Radice, for the conversations, friendship, support and knowledge that you have shared with me. It has been "Priceless".

To my family and friends who have unselfishly allowed me to take time away from them, to continue this project. Especially to my Summer (Time) Chapman, for being my biggest supporter.

Special thanks to Karen Ward of "Gracious Hands" for her Self-Publishing class. Thank you to Diana Davis for her editing of the first edition of "This Week In Black History". None of this would have been possible without your help. To Monwell Floyd, who has always been a GREAT friend.

In Loving Memory of My Sister Paulette T. Price. Thanks for being one of the "Greatest" sisters in the world. You will always be in my thoughts (R.I.P.).

"History is Not What Makes You. You Are What Makes History."

By Willie A. Price

President Barack Obama

Martin Luther King Jr.

About the Author

Many know Willie A. Price as the President of Majadi Enterprises Inc., Property Inspections and Management Training. Some know him as the Housing and Urban Development (HUD) Multi-Family and Public Housing Inspector or the Author and Presenter of Property Management and Maintenance Publications and Workshops.

However, to many he is known as an author, motivational speaker and youth presenter who's workshops and publications are reaching families all over the world. He is the Author of, This Week in Black History, Preparing Your Home for Winter and the "Making Your House your Home" book series, who has been honored and recognized for his work.

Willie A. Price now resides between the cities of Buffalo and Niagara Falls, N.Y. where he is a Real Estate Investor and Entrepreneur. Mr. Price has written numerous articles for local community newspapers on subjects ranging from Black History, Real Estate Investing and Home Inspections for several years.

Mr. Price attended B.U.I.L.D. Academy Elementary School located in Buffalo, N.Y., which he later realized was a blessing that was not appreciated until later in life. The teaching of Black History and positive self-worth was instilled in all of the children at the school on a daily basis.

Following his graduation from the University at Buffalo with a degree in Mental Health, Mr. Price worked part-time as a substitute teacher in the Buffalo Public School System. During his time in the school system he noticed how little knowledge & information was available about African Americans and their contributions to society. This was most apparent during the Black History Month celebrations. At that time students were assigned African American book reports for class. Many of them wrote about the same African Americans: Malcolm X, Martin L. King Jr. and Harriet Tubman. Occasionally some would write about Thurgood Marshall. Mr. Price realized that so many Black and non-Black students had little or no knowledge of the contributions made by African Americans in the world's history. But, he also came to realize that many of the schoolteachers and the parents of those same students were in the same condition.

Several years ago he began writing a weekly article for the Challenger Newspaper entitled: This Week in Black History. He has compiled that information and added additional information to create this book. Mr. Price is a Life Member of Alpha Phi Alpha Fraternity Incorporated (AΦA), Eta Rho Lambda Chapter and a Prince Hall Mason: Eureka Lodge 36 located in Rochester, N.Y.

Introduction

This Week in Black History is a book written for people from all walks of life. You may be young, old, black or white. The purpose of this book is to awaken peoples mind to the contributions of African Americans in the world. The book not only gives information about Blacks and their contributions to the world, it also encourages the reader to ask questions about the person or event, with the hope that they will research those questions, persons or events.

This book is a way to bring a new perspective and ideology to all Americans regardless of their race, creed, color or economic background.

From Kings to Presidents

The purpose of this book is to show that African Americans have made contributions to society every day of the year. It encourages the reader to ask questions about the person or event(s), with the hope that they will utilize libraries and the Internet to find out more about the topic you are researching.

Note

Many of the inventions noted in this book should be researched for the actual invention or part invented. Many items may be listed under the popular category or name of the item invented. The actual invention may be a part or improvement to the invention listed. I make this clarification after being interviewed by a reporter who later disputed every invention and made the statement: "The "Only" thing I ever knew that a Black man invented was the **Peanut**!"

Public Sale of Negroes,
By RICHARD CLAGETT.

On Tuesday, March 5th, 1833 at 1:00 P. M. the following Slaves will be sold at Potters Mart, in Charleston, S. C.

Miscellaneous Lots of Negroes, mostly house servants, some for field work.

Conditions: ½ cash, balance by bond, bearing interest from date of sale. Payable in one to two years to be secured by a mortgage of the Negroes, and appraised personal security. Auctioneer will pay for the papers.

A valuable Negro woman, accustomed to all kinds of house work. Is a good plain cook, and excellent dairy maid, washes and irons. She has four children, one a girl about 13 years of age, another 7, a boy about 5, and an infant 11 months old. 2 of the children will be sold with mother, the others separately, if it best suits the purchaser.

A very valuable Blacksmith, wife and daughters; the Smith is in the prime of life, and a perfect master at his trade. His wife about 27 years old, and his daughters 12 and 10 years old have been brought up as house servants, and as such are very valuable. Also for sale 2 likely young negro wenches, one of whom is 16 the other 13, both of whom have been taught and accustomed to the duties of house servants. The 16 year old wench has one eye.

A likely yellow girl about 17 or 18 years old, has been accustomed to all kinds of house and garden work. She is sold for no fault. Sound as a dollar.

House servants: The owner of a family described herein, would sell them for a good price only, they are offered for no fault whatever, but because they can be done without, and money is needed, He has been offered $1250. They consist of a man 30 to 33 years old, who has been raised in a genteel Virginia family as house servant, Carriage driver etc., in all which he excels. His wife a likely wench of 25 to 30 raised in like manner, as chamber maid, seamstress, nurse etc., their two children, girls of 12 and 4 or 5. They are bright mulattoes, of mild tractable dispositions, unassuming manners, and of genteel appearance and well worthy the notice of a gentleman of fortune needing such.

Also 14 Negro Wenches ranging from 16 to 25 years of age, all sound and capable of doing a good days work in the house or field.

Source unknown

"Let us not forget those who paid the price."

Table of Contents

JANUARY .... 1.

FEBRUARY 7

MARCH 13

APRIL 18

MAY 23

JUNE 28

JULY 33

AUGUST 38

SEPTEMBER 43

OCTOBER 48

NOVEMBER 53

DECEMBER 58

GABRIELLE DOUGLAS 63

ERNESTINE SHEPHERD 64

FRONT COVER 65

BARACK OBAMA 67

GAMES & ACTIVITES 74

ANSWER PAGE 95

BLACK INVENTORS & INVENTIONS 98

REFERENCES 102

JANUARY
Famous Birthdays of the Divine 9

Iota Phi Theta
September 19, 1963

Alpha Kappa Alpha
January 15, 1908

Kappa Alpha Psi
January 5, 1911

Sigma Gamma Rho
November 12, 1922

Alpha Phi Alpha
December 4, 1906

Omega Psi Phi
November 17, 1911

Zeta Phi Beta
January 16, 1920

Phi Beta Sigma
January 9, 1914

Delta Sigma Theta
January 13, 1913

JANUARY

January 1:
1863: The Emancipation Proclamation went into effect. 1996: LaMetta Wynn elected the first Black female Mayor in the state of Iowa. 2006: Byron Brown (AΦA): Officially took office as the first Black Mayor of the city of Buffalo, N.Y.

January 2:
1831: "The Liberator": Abolitionist newspaper, first edition was published in Boston, in the U.S.A. She died on this day at the age of 114 years old.

January 3:
1995: Marion Barry begins his third term as Mayor of Washington, D.C.

January 4:
1943: William L. Dawson was elected as a United States Representative for Illinois. 1971: Congressional Black Caucus was organized. * Where was the Black Caucus organized? 2007: Deval Patrick became the first African American Governor of the State of Massachusetts.

January 5:
1869: Birth of Matilda S. Joyner Jones ("Black Patti"): Performed (singer) in the White House for President Benjamin Harrison. 1911: Kappa Alpha Psi was founded at Indiana University. 1943: Death of George Washington Carver: One of the greatest scientists of all times.

January 6:
1773: Massachusetts's slaves petition for freedom. Who did they have to petition? 2011: Barbara Hillary became the 1st known African American Female to reach the South Pole at age 79. She also was the 1st known to reach the North Pole at age 75.

January 7:
1890: W. B. Purvis Patented the Fountain Pen. 1923: Roland Hayes was acclaimed after performing a Boston recital. 1985: Birth of Lewis Hamilton became the 1st. Black man to win a Formula 1 race. He won the Canadian Grand Prix in Montreal, Canada. What kind of car was he driving in the race? 2013: Meagan Good: Became the 1st Black Female Lead in 30 years on the NBC Network. Her Lead appearance was on the television show "Deception".

January 8:
1811: The first slave revolt in the city of New Orleans took place. 1996: Willie Brown is sworn in as the first Black Mayor of San Francisco, Ca.

January 9:
1866: Fisk University founded, Nashville, TN. 1889: Birth of Beatrice Cannady Taylor: Civil Rights leader. 1914: Phi Beta Sigma Fraternity Inc. was founded at Howard University.

January 10:
1860: Birth of George Washington Carver: Developed over 300 different products from the peanut. 1866: The Georgia Equal Rights Association was organized. 1911: Kappa Alpha Psi Fraternity Inc.: Founded at Indiana University. 1915: Birth of Charles D. Dixon: The first Black to conduct a symphony orchestra.

January 11:
1770: Over 462,000 slaves recorded in the 13 colonies. 1961: Death of Charlotte Hawkins Brown: Converted a run-down church into a 300 acre campus called the Palmer Memorial Institute (1902) in Sadalia, North Carolina.

January 12:
1890: Birth of Mordecai W. Johnson: The first Black President of Howard University. 1952: University of Tennessee admitted its first Black student. 1965: Death of Lorraine V. Hansberry: The first Black author to receive the New York Drama Critics Circle Award, for her play "A Raisin in the Sun".

January 13:
1913: Delta Sigma Theta Sorority Inc.: Founded at Howard University. 1966: Robert C. Weaver nominated secretary of Housing and Urban Development (H.U.D.).

January 14:
1868: The African-American delegates were the majority at South Carolina State Assembly.

January 15:
1881: Birth of William Pickens: The first Black Dean of Morgan State College in Baltimore, MD. 1908: Miner Hall was the site of **Alpha Kappa Alpha Sorority** founding on Howard University campus. 1929: Birth of Dr. Martin L. King jr. (AΦA): Civil Rights Leader. 1965: Birth of Michael "Pinball" Clemons, first African American Canadian Football League Head Coach to win the "92nd Grey Cup" (Team: Toronto Argonauts).

January 16:
1776: Enlistment of freed Blacks into the military. 1920: Zeta Phi Beta Sorority Inc.: Founded at Howard University.

January 17:
1917: Virgin Islands purchased by the U.S. 1955: Marian Anderson: The first Black female on stage at the Metropolitan Opera House. 1964: Birth of Michelle Obama, the 1st Lady and wife of the 1st Black President of the U.S. A. Barack Obama.

January 18:
1856: birth of Dr. Daniel Hale Williams: Performed the first successful heart operation. 1938: Cap B. Collins: Patented the portable electric light.

January 19:
1778: First Black Baptist church organized in Savannah, Georgia. 1856: Biddy Mason: Challenged a California court and won freedom from slavery for her and her family. Birth of John H. Johnson (AΦA): Publisher

January 20:
1778: Andrew Bryan: Became the first Black ordained pastor. *Can you find out for what religion? 2001: General Colin Powell: Became the First African American Secretary of State. 2009: President Barack Obama: Inauguration Day for the First Black President elect of the United States of America.

January 21:
1824: Osai Tutu Kwamina: Defeated the British at Assamaka, Ashanti.

January 22:
1793: Benjamin Banneker: Helped develop the architectural plans for Washington, D.C.

January 23:
1976: Death of Paul Robeson (AΦA): Outstanding scholar, athlete, and actor, best known for his role as "Othello". 1977: First ABC-TV showing of "Roots".

January 24:
1874: Birth of Arthur A. Schomburg: Assembled a priceless collection of Black History at the New York City Public Library. 1918: Lewis H. Latimer: (Inventor) was honored for his contributions and inventions. 1962: Jackie Robinson elected to the Baseball Hall of Fame.

January 25:
1966: Constance B. Motley: First Black woman appointed Federal judge. 1949: Birth of Sheila Johnson, Co-Founder of Black Entertainment Television & the first African American Female Billionaire.

January 26:
1961: Carl T. Rowan: The Journalist receives a position as a White House journalist.

January 27:
1961: Leontyne Price: Made her first appearance with The Metropolitan Opera.

January 28:
1901: Birth of Richard Barthe: Sculptor.

January 29:
1908: Alpha Phi Alpha Fraternity became incorporated. 1977: Andrew Young (AΦA): United Nations appointment confirmed by the U.S. Senate.

January 30:
1865: The 13th Amendment to abolish slavery was presented to Congress.

January 31:
1865: Congress passes the 13th Amendment to abolish slavery. *What roles did Blacks play in the development or implementation of the 13th Amendment?
1919: Birth of Jackie Robinson: He became the first black Major League Baseball (MLB) Player of the modern era. Robinson broke the baseball color line when he debuted with the Brooklyn Dodgers in 1947.

February

Black History Month

In 1926, Carter G. Woodson pioneered the celebration of "Negro History Week", designated for the second week in February, to coincide with marking the birthdays of Abraham Lincoln and Frederick Douglass. The week of recognition became accepted and has been extended as the full month of February, now known as Black History Month.

While working on this Edition of This Week in Black History, I read this message posted by a teacher friend on FB.

My 1st Period Class has 22 students. 13 students are absent from class. 2 of the students showed up on time. The other 7 came in more than 30min late for class. Not one of them completed the assignment handed out. "They say teachers don't care, that's why kids are not learning" SMH!!

Reading this posting just reinforced my motivation to complete this new edition, with the hope that some young person will read it and feel encouraged to make a change in their situation.

FEBRUARY

February 1:
1865: John S. Rock, first African-American lawyer to practice before the U.S. Supreme Court. 1902: Birth of Langston Hughes, one of history's greatest poets. 1995: Robert J. Hollands Jr.: Named the first Black C.E.O. of Ben & Jerry's Homemade Ice cream Company Inc.

February 2:
1897: Alfred L. Cralle patented the Ice Cream Scooper.

February 3:
1868: John Mercer Langston spoke at the Alabama capitol. *Do you know what his topic addressed?

February 4:
1822: Freed African-Americans settled in Liberia, West Africa. 1867: The Peabody Fund was established to aid Blacks with their education. 2007: Lovie Smith (Chicago Bears) and Tony Dungy (Indianapolis Colts), became the first African American head coaches to bring teams to the Super Bowl XLI (41).

February 5:
"National Day of Prayer for the African-American Family".
1934: Birth of Hank Aaron: "Baseball Great", who broke Babe Ruth's home run record.

February 6:
1961: The "Jail-In Movement" began in Rock Hill, N.C. 1993: Death of Arthur Ashe: The first African-American male champion tennis player.

February 7:
1867: Frederick Douglass and a Negro delegation met with President Johnson at the White House. **1916: Birth of Willie C. Fields Sr.:** The first African American to receive a retail liquor license from the New York State Liquor Authority in Niagara County. **1926: Dr. Carter G. Woodson founded Negro History Week (Feb. 1-7).** 1976: "Negro History Week" was expanded to the entire month of February: "Black History Month. 2007: Death of Willye White. The 1st woman to compete for the U.S. in 5 Olympic Games (1956, 1960, 1964, 1968, 1972).

February 8:
1951: Private Edward O. Cleaborn: Awarded the "Distinguished Service Cross", for his military service.

February 9:
1964: Arthur Ashe (tennis player): First African-American on U.S. Davis Cup team. 1965: Dr. Martin L. King Jr. met with President Johnson at the White House. 1995: Bernard A. Harris, Jr.: First African-American to walk in space (space shuttle Discovery). *Can you find the full names of the Presidents whose names were Johnson?

February 10:
1780: Seven Blacks challenged the U.S. constitution on taxation without representation. *How successful was their challenge? 1854: Birth of Joseph C. Price: Founder and the first President of Livingstone College. 1992: Death of Alex Haley: Author of the novel "Roots".

February 11:
1933: Lois Gardella: Selected as the original "Aunt Jemima" for the famous pancake brand. 1990: Nelson Mandela: Released from prison after 27 years as a South African political prisoner.

February 12:
1909: The National Association for the Advancement of Colored People (N.A.A.C.P.) was founded. *Do you know who the founders were?

February 13:
1746: Birth of Absalom Jones: First Black Protestant minister. 1873: Birth of Emmett J. Scott: Black businessman and administrator: All of his primary business ventures were managed by Blacks and served only Black customers. 1920: Baseball Negro League was founded. 1922: Death of Fannie M. Richards: Detroit's first Black Public School teacher: She was also the founder and first president of the Phyllis Wheatley Home for Aged Black Women.

February 14:
1817: Birth of Frederick Douglass, Tuckahoe, MD. 1876: The Augusta Institute, which later became Morehouse College, opened in Atlanta, Ga.

February 15:
1957: The Southern Christian Leadership Conference (S.C.L.C.) organization was founded. *Who were the organizers and why did they organize?

February 16:
1874: Frederick Douglass elected President of Freedman's Bank & Trust Company. * Where was this located?

February 17:
1923: Bessie Smith: The first Black female to make a recording for Columbia Records.

February 18:
1688: First formal protest against slavery took place. * Where did the protest take place and who were the organizers?

February 19:
1790: George Bridgetower: Musician: Made his first London appearance. 1919: Pan-African Congress organized by W.E.B. DuBois (ΑΦΑ).

February 20:
1895: Death of Frederick Douglass (AΦA).

February 21:
1965: Death of Malcolm X (El Haji Malik El): Assassinated in New York City.

February 22:
1967: Adam Clayton Powell (AΦA): Stripped of his seniority. *Do you know what seniority, where this took place and why?

February 23:
1868: W.E.B. DuBois (AΦA): Born and died on this day in 1963, at age 95.

February 24:
1811: Birth of Daniel A. Payne (Educator): The first Black to become a college President. *What college did he become President?

February 25:
1870: Hiram Revels: Elected first Black in U.S. Senate. *What state did he represent? 2002: Venus Williams becomes the first African American to hold the #1 ranking in tennis.

February 26:
1930: The play "Green Pastures" opened in a New York City theater.

February 27:
1844: The continent of the Dominican Republic was established on this date. 1903: Birth of Marian Anderson: The first Black to ever appear on the stage of the Metropolitan Opera House.

February 28:
1842: Charles Lenox Remond testified before the Massachusetts House Committee.
*What did he testify about?
_____

February 29: (Leap Year, every 4 years):
　　　　"Make your own Black History Day event(s)"
_____
_____
_____
_____
_____

MARCH

Crispus Attucks

Crispus Attucks was an American slave, merchant seaman and dockworker of Wampanoag and African descent. He was the first person shot to death by British redcoats during the Boston Massacre, in Boston, Massachusetts.

Two major sources of eyewitness testimony about the Boston Massacre, both published in 1770, did not refer to Attucks as a "Negro," or "black" man; it appeared that Bostonians accepted him as mixed race. Historians disagree on whether Crispus Attucks was a free man or an escaped slave; but agree that he was of Wampanoag and African descent.

In the early nineteenth century, as the Abolitionist movement gained momentum in Boston, supporters lauded Attucks as a black American who played a heroic role in the history of the United States

MARCH

March 1:
1875: President Grant signed Civil Rights Law. 1927: Birth: Harry Belafonte: Singer, Actor and Civil Rights Activist.

March 2:
1807: Congress enacted law ending African Slave Trade. 1867: Howard University was chartered.

March 3:
1865: Freedman's Bureau established. * Who established it? What was their mission? 1886: Robert Flemming Jr. patented the guitar.

March 4:
1875: Birth: Garrett A. Morgan: Inventor of the Automatic Traffic Signal and the Gas Mask. 1875: Blanch Bruce elected United States Senator for Mississippi.

March 5:
1770: Death: Crispus Attucks: The first Black killed during the "American Revolution", in Boston Mass.

March 6:
1857: The U.S. Supreme Court ruled on the Dred Scott Decision. *Can you explain what this decision was?

March 7:
1539: Esteban explored southwestern part of U.S.

March 8:
1876: Senate refused to seat P.B.S. Pinchback. *Why did they do this?

March 9:
1961: Clifton Wharton sworn in as Ambassador to Norway. 1995: Leon Day, a pitcher in the former Negro League, is elected to the "Baseball Hall of Fame".

March 10:
1845: Birth of Hallie Q. Brown, educator and women's Civil Rights messenger. 1910: Robert L. Vann: Published first edition of "The Pittsburgh Courier." 1913: Death: Harriet Tubman: Underground Railroad Leader.

March 11:
1959: The play "Raisin In The Sun" opened on Broadway. 1971: Death: Whitney Young: Director of the National Urban League. 1969: Birth of Terrence Howard: Actor.

March 12:
1770: The first Army paycheck was issued to a slave named, William Kitchen. 1955: Death: Charlie Parker: Jazz Musician. 1960: Birth of Courtney Vance: Actor. 1964 Malcolm X: Resigned from the Nation of Islam.

March 13:
1865: A bill was issued authorizing slaves as soldiers in the Confederate Army. 1968: Death of Meta Vaux Warrick Fuller: A celebrated sculptress.

March 14:
1889: Menelik became ruler of Abyssinia. 1977: Death of Fannie L. Hammer: Freedom fighter.

March 15:
1947: John Lee became the first Black officer in the Navy.

March 16:
1827: The "Freedom's Journal": The first Black Newspaper founded. 1846 - Rebecca Cole, second Black female physician in America was born.

March 17:
1896: C.B. Scott: Patents the street sweeper.

March 18:
1947: Louis Lautier: The first Black Congressional newsman.

March 19:
1794: "Jay's Treaty" took effect. *What was this treaty?

March 20:
1852: Landmark novel "Uncle Tom's Cabin" was published. 1957: Birth of Shelton Jackson **"Spike" Lee** an American film director, producer, writer, and actor. 1965: The 54 mile "Civil Rights March" took place from Selma to Montgomery, Al.

March 21:
1955: Death of Walter White: A past N.A.A.C.P. leader. *Why was he important?

March 22:
1941: The Tuskegee Airmen Pilot Training Program started. *Where was it started and how successful was it?

March 23:
1873: The abolishment of slavery in Puerto Rico went into effect.

March 24:
1865: Black troops enlisted in large numbers into the Confederate military service. 1886: Death of Justin Holland: Guitarist and publisher of "Holland's Modern Method for the Guitar".

March 25:
1975: Massachusetts's postage stamp honors Salem Poor. *Who or what are the Salem Poor?

March 26:
1833: Birth of Joseph C. Corbin: Known for his intellect, earning several college degrees and mastering seven different languages. 1872: Thomas J. Martin patented the Fire Extinguisher. 1911: William H. Lewis became U.S. Assistant Attorney General.

March 27:
1501: Black seamen, soldiers, and explorers brought to America. *Where did they come from and who brought them?

March 28:
1958: Death of William C. Handy: Known as "Father of the Blues"
1984: Death of Benjamin E. Mays: An authority on Black Religion, served 27 years as President of Morehouse College.

March 29:
1815: Napoleon Bonapart, the Emperor of France banned the slave trade. 1918: Birth of Pearl Bailey: singer and actress. 1974: Death of Duke Ellington: Big Band conductor.

March 30:
1870: The 15th Amendment was passed giving Blacks the right to vote.

March 31:
1880: Birth of J.E. Walker: The founder of "Universal Life's" *What is "Universal Life's"? 1995: Shirley Jackson: The first woman, Black or White to be nominated to the post of Chairperson for the Nuclear Regulations Commission.

APRIL

Robert L. Johnson

Robert L. Johnson (born April 8, 1946) is an American business magnate best known for being the founder of television network Black Entertainment Television (BET), and is also its former chairman and chief executive officer. Johnson is currently chairman and founder of RLJ Development and former majority owner of the Charlotte Bobcats, a National Basketball Association franchise along with rapper Nelly and NBA legend and current majority owner Michael Jordan. In 2001, Johnson became the first African American billionaire, and the first black person to be listed on any of Forbes world's rich list (excluding black Canadian billionaire Michael Lee-Chin who first appeared on the list the same year, who is of mixed black and Chinese ancestry).

Michael Lee-Chin

APRIL

April 1: "April Fool's Day"
1950: Death of Dr. Charles Drew: Developer of blood plasma. Dr. Drew died after an auto accident, when transported to a white hospital. They refused to give him (his own discovery) blood plasma.

April 2:
1796: Toussaint L' Ouverture commanded French Forces at St. Domingo. 1932: Death of Bill Pickett: The greatest Black cowboy that ever lived: The first Black cowboy admitted to the National Rodeo Hall of Fame.

April 3:
1950: Death of Carter G. Woodson. He was a historian, journalist and author. He was known as the father of black history. * What was he famous for?

April 4:
1968: Martin Luther King Jr. (AΦA): Assassinated in Memphis, Tenn.

April 5:
1856: Booker T. Washington, born a slave in the state of Virginia. *Where in Virginia was he born? 1937: Birth of General Colin Powell, First Black Secretary of State.

April 6:
1798: Birth of James P. Beckwourth: Explored the West years before J.C. Fremont. 1909: Matthew Henson co-discovered the North Pole.

April 7:
1975: Frank Robinson named the first Black Cleveland Indians baseball team manager. 2009-2012: Theodore Long, first African American General Manager for World Wrestling Entertainment.

April 8:
1974: Hank Aaron: Broke Babe Ruth's baseball home run record with 715 hits.
1946: Birth of Robert L. Johnson, founder of Black Entertainment Television and first Black Billionaire.

April 9:
1866: The Civil Rights Bill passed over a Presidential veto. *Who was the President that vetoed the bill? 1979: Keisha Knight Pulliam: Actress best known for her role as "Rudy" on "The Cosby Show".

April 10:
1833: London audience acclaimed Ira Aldridge for playing the role of "Othello"
1947: Jackie Robinson named the first Black baseball player in the National Baseball League. *What team did he play for?

April 11:
1947: Jackie Robinson played his first professional baseball game for the National Baseball league. 1955: Roy Wilkinson appointed N.A.A.C.P. Executive secretary.

April 12:
1983: Harold Washington: The first Black elected mayor of Chicago.

April 13:
1854: Birth of Lucy C. Laney: Educator. *Why is she important?

April 14:
1775: The first Abolitionist Society was organized in Philadelphia. *Who were the organizers? 1964: Sidney Poitier: The first Black male to win an Oscar Award.

April 15:
1960: The Student Nonviolent Coordinator Committee (S.N.C.C.) was organized at Shaw University. *Where is Shaw and who were the organizers?

April 16:
1869: Ebenezer Don Carlos Bassett named United States Ambassador to Haiti. He was the first Black Diplomat for the United States.

April 17:
1758: Francis Williams, a Blackman published a book of Latin poems. 1990: Death of Ralph Abernathy. *Who was Mr. Abernathy?

April 18:
1818: Native American Indians and Blacks defeated in the Battle of Sewanee. *Where is Sewanee? Who defeated them?

April 19:
1775: Black and White Minutemen fought together at Lexington and Concord. *Where is Lexington and Concord? Who did they fight?

April 20:
1866: Fisk University opened in Nashville, T.N.

April 21:
1565: Black explorers along with the Spaniard Menendez discovered St. Augustine, Florida.

April 22:
1970: Student protest took place at Yale University to support the Black Panther Party.

April 23:
1872: Charlotte E. Ray: The first Black woman admitted to Bar Association. 1918: The National Urban League was founded. *Where was it founded?

April 24:
1950: The first Black student was enrolled into the University of North Carolina. *Who was this student?

April 25:
1941: The "Fair Employment Practices Commission" was established. *Who established it and why was it established?

April 26:
1966: Private Milton L. Olive, III, awarded Medal of Honor posthumously.
1988: Death of Dr. Frederick Douglass Patterson: Founded the George Washington Carver Foundation. *Where was it founded?

April 27:
1961: Sierra Leone, West Africa granted independence, after 150 years under British rule.

April 28:
1847: George B. Vashon: The first Black man admitted to the New York State Bar Association.

April 29:
1899: Birth of Edward Kennedy "Duke" Ellington (AΦA), in Washington D.C. He was known as the father of the "Big Band" and "Bee Bop" era.

April 30:
1982: Birth of Buffalo's own Erika Copeland: Erika's goal was to be the first Black female on the U.S. Ski Team. * Did she accomplish her goal? 1983: Memphis Blues honored at the Smithsonian Institute.

MAY

Tia Norfleet

Tia Norfleet (born May 1, 1988 in Suffolk, Virginia) is an African-American drag racing and stock car racing driver. The daughter of NASCAR driver Bobby Norfleet, she is the first African-American woman to receive a NASCAR racing license. As of 2012 Norfleet competes in late model races at short tracks throughout the southeastern United States

Norfleet's interest in racing began at the age of 7, when her father, NASCAR driver Bobby Norfleet, doubled the battery power of a Hot Wheels Barbie car to increase its speed. Norfleet's racing career began at age 14, when she began competing in kart racing events; she went on to a successful career in drag racing at the local and regional level, where she won 37 of 52 events she competed in.

In 2000 Norfleet switched to stock car racing, competing in Bandolero cars, and then moving to late model stock car racing on short tracks starting with the 2004 racing season; she became the first female African-American driver to receive a NASCAR racing license.

Norfleet competes in local late model events at tracks near her Augusta, Georgia home, starting her Late Model career in 2004. She plans to compete in NASCAR national touring series competition starting in the summer of 2012, and is operating a grassroots funding initiative to finance her racing career.

MAY

May 1:
1867: Howard University was chartered by congress. 1988: Birth of Tia Norfleet: The first African American woman NASCAR Driver.

May 2:
1968: The Poor Peoples March to Washington D.C. began.

May 3:
1947: The Supreme Court struck down "Restrictive Covenants". *What is this covenant? 1978: Ernest N. Moral (ΑΦΑ): Elected the first Black Mayor of New Orleans LA.

May 4:
1897: J.H. Smith patents the lawn sprinkler. 1961: Free rides were provided to Black patrons during the protest of segregated bus terminals. *Where did this take place?

May 5:
1841: Birth of William H. Crogman, a noted Classical scholar.

May 6:
"Civil Rights Act" started. 1995: Ron Kirk elected first black mayor of a major city in Texas (Dallas Texas).

May 7:
1800: Jean Baptiste Pointe DuSable: Sold his entire wealth (land, business, home, etc.) for $1,200. He was known as the "Father" of the nation's second largest city: This city later became Chicago, Ill. 1963: Birmingham protest crisis. *What was the crisis?

May 8:
1970: The "Chicago Seven" Panther indictment dropped. *Why were they indicted?

May 9:
1862: Slaves in Georgia, Florida, and South Carolina were freed. 1995: Nat Glover: elected the first Black Sheriff, in the state of Florida, for Jacksonville, Florida.

May 10:
1854: Elizabeth Taylor Greenfield sang before Queen Victoria. 1968: Lewis H. Latimer Public School dedicated in Brooklyn N.Y. He was the only Black man assisting Thomas Edison develop the light bulb.

May 11:
1865: Blacks demanded "Equal Rights" & voting ballots in Norfolk, VA.

May 12:
1871: "Sit-In" protest staged in Louisville, Kentucky. *Who were the protestors and why were they protesting? 1963: Medgar Evers assassinated in Jackson, MS. *What role did he play in the "Civil Rights" movement?

May 13:
1914: Birth of Joe Louis: Heavyweight Boxing Champion.

May14:
1880: Birth of Leslie Pickney Hill: Renowned scholar and educator. 1888: Abolition of slavery in Brazil.

May 15:
1791: Civil Rights granted to free Mulattos in French colonies. *What is a Mulatto? 1832: Birth of Mary Fields: Freight hauler, laundress, restaurant owner, and the second female and first Black woman to drive a United States mail coach.

May 16:
1963: Theodore K. Lawless, dermatologist, honored in Chicago. 1967: The city of Lynn, Massachusetts honored Jan E. Matzeliger, who designed and patented a machine, which automatically stitched the leather of the shoe to the sole.

May 17:
1954: U.S. Supreme Court made "Brown vs. Board of Education" decision. *What is the importance of this decision?

May 18:
1848: Death of William A. Leidesdorff: The first Black millionaire in America. He built San Francisco's first hotel, opened the state of California's first public school, and also introduced the first steamboat and the first official horse race to the state of California. 1896: Plessy vs. Ferguson decision. *Why was this important?

May 19:
1930: Birth of Lorraine V. Hansberry: Authored the play "Raisin in the Sun". 1976: Gwendolyn Brooks inducted into National Institute of Arts & Letters. 2006: Sophia Danenberg, first African American to reach the peak of Mount Everest.

May 20:
1925: Birth of Malcolm X, born Malcolm Little, Omaha, NE. 1958: Robert N.C. Nix elected to Congress for the state of Pennsylvania.

May 21:
1891: Peter Jackson fought a 61 round draw (tie) with a white boxer. *Who was the White Boxer?

May 22:
1863: Sgt. William H. Carney received a Congressional Medal. 1863: The U.S. government authorized the first Black military troop. 1967: Death of Langston Hughes: Famous poet and playwright.

May 23:
1863: Assault on Port Hudson. *Where is Port Hudson and why was it assaulted?

May 24:
1854: Lincoln University was founded in the state of Pennsylvania (*Where?). 1974: Death of Duke Ellington: "Big Band" musician and conductor at age 75.

May 25:
1849: Birth of Thomas Green Bethune: "Blind Tom", musical genius. 1937: Death of Henry Ossawa Tanner: First Black artist of international fame.1951: Willie Mays entered Major League Baseball.

May 26:
1799: Birth of Alexander S. Pushkin (Black Russian): Became Russia's greatest poet. 1965: U.S. Senate passed Voting Rights Bill.

May 27:
1870: Michael Howard: First Black admitted into the West Point Academy.

May 28:
Sojourner Truth attended Women's Rights Convention. *Where was the convention held and what year?

May 29:
1858: William Wells Brown: Published the first Black play: "The Escape". *What was the play about? 1950: American Bowling Congress eliminated racial designations for members.

May 30:
1909: First conference of National Negro Committee (now N.A.A.C.P.). *Where was the conference held?

May 31:
1955: The U.S. Supreme Court ordered school integration decision.

JUNE

Lewis Hamilton

Lewis Carl Davidson Hamilton is the 2008 Formula One World Champion. Hamilton was born in Stevenage, Hertfordshire (England). In December 1995, at the age of ten, he approached McLaren team president Ron Dennis at the Auto Sport Awards ceremony and told him, "I want to race for you one day." Less than three years later McLaren and Mercedes-Benz signed him to their Young Driver Support Program. After winning the British Formula Renault, Formula Three Euro-series, and GP2 championships on his way up the racing career ladder, he drove for McLaren in 2007, making his Formula One debut 12 years after his initial encounter with Dennis.

Hamilton's contract for the McLaren driver development program made him the youngest ever driver to secure a contract which later resulted in a Formula One drive. Coming from a mixed background, with a black father and white mother, Hamilton is often labeled "the first black driver in Formula One", although Willy T. Ribbs **tested** an F1 car in 1986. He is also the first driver of black heritage to win a major race at Indianapolis Motor Speedway in any discipline.

In his first season in Formula One, Hamilton set numerous records, while finishing second in the 2007 Formula One Championship, just one point behind Kimi Räikkönen. He won the World Championship the following season.

JUNE

June 1:
1875: James A. Healey: Ordained a Catholic Bishop.

June 2:
1868: Birth of John Hope: the first Black President of Morehouse College in 1913. 1943: 99th Pursuit Squadron's first combat mission. *Who were these men and where did they come from?

June 3:
1884: Granville T. Woods patented the steam boiler furnace. 1906: Birth of Josephine Baker: Famous singer and dancer. *How many children did Josephine Baker have?

June 4:
1665: The first Baptist Church in the United States was founded. * Who was the founder and where was it located? 1895: Joseph Lee: Patented the bread-crumbing machine.

June 5:
1851: Dr. James W.C. Pennington purchased his freedom for $150.00. He was the first Black man to receive a Doctor of Divinity degree. *Where did he receive his degree? 1907: Jockey Jimmy Lee: Made racing history as a Black jockey.

June 6:
1831: The first annual "People of Color" convention was held in Philadelphia, Pa. 1968: Robert F. Kennedy assassinated, considered "A President for the People". Millions of Black people mourned his death.

June 7:
1892: G.T. Sampson: Patented the clothes dryer. 1946: U.S. Supreme Court banned discrimination in inter-state travel. 1996: Vaddrick Parker, 17, graduated from Southeast H.S., Hobgood, N.C., without missing a day of school in 13 years (Kinder-H.S.).

June 8:
1953: The Supreme Court outlawed racial discrimination in Washington, D.C.

June 9:
1877: Birth of Meta Vaux Warrick Fuller: A gifted and celebrated sculptor.

June 10:
1938: Death of Arthur A. Schomburg: He assembled a priceless collection of Black history that is available at the New York City's Public Library. 2001: Birth of Natasha "Sasha" Obama, the youngest daughter of President Barack & Michelle Obama. *2007: Lewis Hamilton became the 1st. African American to win a Formula 1 race. He won the Canadian Grand Prix in Montreal, Canada. What kind of car was he driving in the race?

June 11:
1911: Marcus Garvey founded The Universal Negro Improvement Association.

June 12:
1964: Nelson Mandela sentenced to life in prison. *How long did he stay in prison?

June 13:
1868: Oscar J. Dunn, ex-slave, installed as Lieutenant Governor of Louisiana. 1908: Death of Thomas "Blind Tom" Bethune: A musical wonder. 1967: Thurgood Marshall named to the U.S. Supreme Court.

June 14:
1952: Dr. Harold D. West president of Meharry Medical College, Nashville, TN.

June 15:
1877: Henry O. Flipper graduated from the West Point Academy.

June 16:
1804: Dessalines was declared emperor of Haiti.

June 17:
1938: Death of James Weldon Johnson: First Black lawyer admitted to the Florida bar and the author of the Black National Anthem, "Lift Every Voice And Sing".
1972: Frank Willis (security guard) discovered the Watergate break-in.

June 18:
1863: William H. Carney earned the highest Army medal. *What is the highest Army medal?

June 19:
"Juneteenth": commemoration of the Emancipation of slavery in Texas.
1864: Sailor Joachim Pease earned Congressional Medal.

June 20:
1894: Birth of Lloyd A. Hall: A pioneering industrial food chemist, who developed curing salts for the processing and preserving of meats. 1943: Congress of Racial Equality (C.O.R.E.) founded.

June 21:
1821: African Methodist Episcopal Church organized in New York City. 1859: Birth of Henry O. Tanner: The first Black artist of international fame. 1925: Death of Peter H. Clark: The first Black Socialist in the United States.

June 22:
1897: William Barry patents the postmarking and canceling postal system.

June 23:
1863-1880 Black recruits started reporting to Pennsylvania army camps.

June 24:
1877: Clinton Freaves, army soldier, cited for valor. 1988: Atlanta University and Clark College merge to become Clark Atlanta University. 2005: Jeanine Menze, first African American woman U.S. Coast Guard aviator.

June 25:
1876: Isaiah Dorman, (Black man) first to die in the "Indian-United States" battle.

June 26:
1900: Birth of Rufus E. Clement: Great leader in education, and past President of Atlanta University. 1950: American Medical Association seats first Black Convention delegate. 1959: Prince Edward County, Virginia abandoned public school system.

June 27:
1935: A. Phillip Randolph named the President of the first Black labor union. 1939: Frederick Jones patented the Ticket Dispensing Machine. 2007: Barrington Irving became the youngest person to complete a solo flight around the world at the age of 23, from a plane he built with used parts.

June 28:
1770: The Philadelphia school for Blacks opened by Quakers. *What type of school did they open?

June 29:
1870: J.W. Smith authored "The Colored Cadet Hardships at West Point".

June 30:
1917: Birth of singer Lena Horne.

JULY

Jackie Robinson

Jack Roosevelt "Jackie" Robinson (January 31, 1919 – October 24, 1972) was an American baseball player who became the first black Major League Baseball (MLB) player of the modern era. Robinson broke the baseball color line when he debuted with the Brooklyn Dodgers in 1947. The example of his character and unquestionable talent challenged the traditional basis of segregation, which then marked many other aspects of American life, and contributed significantly, to the Civil Rights Movement.

In addition to his cultural impact, Robinson had an exceptional baseball career. Over ten seasons, he played in six World Series and contributed to the Dodgers' 1955 World Championship. He was selected for six consecutive All-Star Games from 1949 to 1954, was the recipient of the inaugural MLB Rookie of the Year Award in 1947, and won the National League Most Valuable Player Award in 1949—the first black player so honored. Robinson was inducted into the Baseball Hall of Fame in 1962. In 1997, Major League Baseball "universally" retired his uniform number, 42, across all major league teams; the first pro athlete in any sport to be so honored. Since that time, Major League Baseball has adopted a new annual tradition, "Jackie Robinson Day," in which *all* players on *all* teams wear #42.

Robinson was also known for his pursuits outside the baseball diamond. He was the first black television analyst in Major League Baseball, and the first black vice-president of a major American corporation. Robinson was posthumously awarded the Presidential Medal of Freedom and the Congressional Gold Medal.

JULY

July 1:
1870: James W. Smith: Entered the West Point Military Academy.

July 2:
1872: Elijah "Real" McCoy: Received a patent for the first automatic lubricator. 1908: Birth of Thurgood Marshall: First Black Supreme Court Justice. 1964: Civil Rights Bill passed.

July 3:
Jackie Robinson named to the Baseball Hall of Fame.

July 4: "Independence Day"
1881: Tuskegee University founded. 1998: Birth of Malia Ann Obama, the oldest daughter of President Barack & Michelle Obama.

July 5:
1892: Andrew J. Beard patented the rotary steam engine. 1904: George E. Taylor nominated for President of the United States.

July 6:
1854: The Republican Party was organized to oppose slavery. * Who was the organizer (s)? 1971: Henry Sampson invented the Cellular Telephone.

July 7:
1948: Cleveland Indians (Baseball) signed Leroy (Satchel) Paige. *What position did he play?

July 8:
1924: DeHart Hubbard won an Olympic Victory. *What event did he win?

July 9:
1966: N.A.A.C.P. disassociates from "Black Power" doctrine.

July 10:
1893: Daniel H. Williams performs the world's first successful open heart surgery.

July 11:
1905: Niagara Movement founded by W.E.B. DuBois. *What is the Niagara Movement and why was it important?

July 12:
1936: Cornelius Johnson set world high jump record. *How high did he jump?
1949: Frederick Jones patented the Starter Generator and the Air condition.

July 13:
1787: Slavery banned in the Northwest Territory. *Who banned it?

July 14:
1955: The George W. Carver National Monument was dedicated in Joplin, Missouri. This was the first national park to honor an African American.

July 15:
1779: Pompey Lamb, noted Black spy, aided war effort. * Which War?

July 16:
1944: Charles R. Drew awarded the Spingarn Medal. *What does the Spingarn Medal honor? 1974: Robinne Lee: Actress.

July 17:
1862: The U.S. Congress approved the arming of Blacks in the military.

July 18:
1905: Granville Woods patented the railway brake.

July 19:
1960: Wilma Rudolph set the 200m-dash record at the Olympics. *Which Olympics did she compete?

July 20:
1848: Women's Rights Convention aided Anti-Slavery cause. 1962: Birth of W. A. Price, real estate investor, entrepreneur and the author of "This Week in Black History. 1967: Black Power Conference opened in Newark New Jersey.

July 21:
1893: Birth of Charles Johnson: Scholar and past President of Fisk University. 1896: Mary C. Terrel organized the National Association of Colored Women.

July 22:
1963: Floyd Paterson lost boxing match to Sonny Liston.

July 23:
1891: Birth of Louis T. Wright. The first Black physician to be appointed to a hospital staff position and later appointed to head a New York City hospital. *What Hospital? 1965: Martin L. King Jr. conducted a civil rights campaign in Chicago.

July 24:
1826: Ira Aldridge: Black actor made debut in London as "Othello". Charles Bush became a Page for the U.S. Supreme Court, the same year.

July 25:
1941: F.E.P.C. formed by executive order. *What is F.E.P.C.?

July 26:
1847: A young African American man from Virginia named Joseph Jenkins Roberts declared the colony of Liberia, West Africa, an independent Republic.

July 27:
1948: Legal basis established for desegregation of Armed forces. 1980: A. P. Abourne discovered a way to refine coconut oil. 1996: Alice Hawthorne, killed in the Olympic Park bombing, during the 1996 Olympics held in Atlanta, Ga.

July 28:
1868: 14th Amendment ratified. *What did it amend?

July 29:
1895: The First National Conference of Colored Women Convention was held.
*Where was it held?

July 30:
1970: Lou Lomax: Author of "The Hate That Produced", killed in auto accident.
*What was his book about?

July 31:
1921: Birth of Whitney Young Jr., past Urban League Executive Director.

AUGUST

Jesse Owens

He participated in the 1936 Summer Olympics in Berlin, Germany, where he achieved international fame by winning four gold medals: one each in the 100 meters, the 200 meters, the long jump, and as part of the 4x100 meter relay team.

Usain Bolt

He is the first man to hold both the 100m and 200m world records. Along with his teammates, he also set the world record in the 4×100m relay. He was the first to achieve a "double, double" by winning 100m and 200m titles at consecutive Olympics (2008 and 2012), and topped this through the first "double triple" (including 4x100m relays).

AUGUST

August 1:
1895: Birth of Benjamin E. Mays, Minister, Scholar and past President of Morehouse College. (27 YRS.). 1996: Michael Johnson became the first person to win the 200m and 400m in the same Olympic Games (Atlanta 1996).

August 2:
1924: Birth of author James Baldwin in New York City. 1996: Olympic Park Bombing took place in Atlanta, Ga.

August 3:
1800: Gabriel Prosser leads slave revolt in Richmond, Va.
1908: Allenworth Township established in California for former slaves. *Who established the township?

August 4:
1810: Abolitionist Robert Purvis was born. 1961: **Barack Obama** was born: First Black President (44th) of the United States 2008. He was re-elected to the Presidency in 2012.

August 5:
1864: Gunner: John Lawson earned a Congressional medal. *What branch of the military did he serve in?

August 6:
1965: President Johnson signed the Voting Rights Bill.

August 7:
1904: Dr. Ralph Bunche, a United Nations representative received the Nobel Peace Prize.

August 8:
1965: The Voting Rights Bill passed.

August 9:
1936: Jesse Owens wins four Gold medals at the Berlin Olympic Games. *What events did he win the medals? 1961: James B. Parsons appointed to Federal District Court.

August 10:
1965: Thurgood Marshall named the Solicitor General. 1984: Carl Lewis wins four Gold Medals in the Los Angeles Olympic Games. General Colin Powell is nominated chairman, Joint Chiefs of Staff (The first African American).

August 11:
1974: Dr. Martin L. King Jr. picture is hung in the Georgia State Capital.

August 12:
1922: Frederick Douglass Memorial home was dedicated in Washington, D.C.

August 13:
1892: The first issue of the "Afro-American" newspaper was distributed. *Where was it published? 1982: Birth of Shani Davis, first African American Individual (2006) Winter Olympic Gold medal winner (1,000 meter speed skating).

August 14:
1862: President Lincoln addressed an all-Black audience at the White House.

August 15:
1817: Birth of George Washington a Black man was the founder of the city Centralia, Washington.

August 16:
1987: Death of scholar Charles H. Wesley (AφA).

August 17:
1938: Henry Armstrong won the World Lightweight Boxing title. *Was he the first Black man to win this title?

August 18:
1963: James Meredith: The first Black graduate from the University of Mississippi.

August 19:
1884: M.C. Harvey: Inventor patented the lantern.

August 20:
1619-20: The export of the first Black slaves from Africa to Jamestown, Va.

August 21:
1831: Nat Turner led a Slave revolt. *Where did the revolt take place? 1986: Birth of Usain Bolt a Jamaican sprinter widely regarded as the fastest person ever. He is the first man to hold both the 100 meters and 200 meters world records. Along with his teammates, he also set the world record in the 4×100 meters relay. He is the reigning Olympic champion in these three events, the first man to win six Olympic gold medals in sprinting, and a five-time World champion. He was the first to achieve a "double, double" by winning 100 m and 200 m titles at consecutive Olympics (2008 and 2012), and topped this through the first "double triple" (including 4x100m relays).

August 22:
1843: Henry Highland Garnet called a General Slave strike.

August 23:
1796: The A.M.E. Church Incorporated. *Where was it incorporated?

August 24:
1950: Edith Sampson appointed alternate delegate to the United Nations.

August 25:
1862: 5,000 Slaves were armed by the Secretary of War. 1996: Eldrick "Tiger" Woods becomes the first **PERSON** (Black or White) to win the U.S. Amateur Golf Tournament, three years in a row.

August 26:
1943: William L. Dawson elected Democratic Party Vice President. 1993: Birth of Lauren Keyana "KeKe" Palmer, started her career as a child Actress and later singer.

August 27:
1963: W.E.B. DuBois died (AφA).

August 28:
1963: Anniversary of historic "March on Washington". Martin L. King Jr. delivers "I Have a Dream" speech. 2008: **Barack Obama** became the First African American Nominee for President of the United States, representing a Major political party. *Which major political party did he represent?

August 29:
1977: Lou Brock sets Major League baseball's stolen base record.
1997: Birthday of Andrea Johnson (Rochester, N.Y.) who has won the National Frederick Douglass Oratorical competition in Washington, D.C., 3 consecutive years (2004-2007).

August 30:
1983: Guion Bluford: The first Black Astronaut to travel into space. * Do you know the name of the space shuttle?

August 31:
1836: Henry Blair: Patented a cotton-planting machine.

SEPTEMBER

Sebrina Philpart-Brunson

On September 20, 2008 Sebrina Philpart-Brunson became one of the few women to officiate a regular season male college football game. She performed as a line judge in the Stillman College vs. Tuskegee University, making her way as the first woman to officiate a NCAA Division II, Southern Intercollegiate Athletic Conference's (SIAC) college football game.

Her ultimate goals however is to wear the black and white uniform as an official in the NFL.

Michael Johnson

Johnson currently holds the world and Olympic records in the 400 m. He is the only male athlete in history to win both the 200m dash and 400m dash events at the same Olympics, a feat he accomplished at the 1996 Summer Olympics in Atlanta.

SEPTEMBER

September 1:
1977: Death of Ethel Waters at age 77. *What was she famous for?

September 2:
1969: The first outbreak of Black civil disorder in Hartford, Connecticut.

September 3:
1886: Birth of Alain Locke: The first Black Rhode Scholar. *What is a Rhode Scholar?

September 4:
1962: New Orleans Catholic schools became integrated. 1981: Birth of Beyonce Knowles, first African American woman to win the ASCAP Pop Music Songwriter of the Year award.

September 5:
1960: Leopold Sedar Senghor: Elected President of Senegal.

September 6:
1848: Frederick Douglass: Elected president of the National Black Political Convention in Cleveland, Ohio.

September 7:
1954: Washington, D.C. and Baltimore, Md., Public Schools became integrated.

September 8:
1907: Negro League baseball star Buck Leonard was born.

September 9:
1963: Iota Phi Theta Fraternity Inc. was founded at Morgan State University. 1968: Arthur Ashe jr. the first Black person to win the U.S. Open Tennis Championship.

September 10:
1855: John Mercer Langston was elected township clerk of Brownhelm, Ohio. He became the first Black to hold the elected office in the U.S.

September 11:
1974: Haile Selassie I: Removed from the Ethiopian throne. 2001: The Twin Towers of New York City destroyed by terrorist in U.S. passenger airplanes. Several Blacks died on the planes and in the towers.

September 12:
1787: First Black Masonic Lodge organized. *Where was it organized?

September 13:
1663: The first serious slave conspiracy took place in Virginia. 1967: Birth of Michael Johnson has won four Olympic gold medals and eight World Championships gold medals. He currently holds the world and Olympic records in the 400m . 1969: Birth of Tyler Perry is an American actor, director, screenwriter, playwright, producer, author, and songwriter

September 14:
1940: Selective Service Act went into effect. Several Blacks were inducted into the military, due to this Act.

September 15:
1963: Birmingham, Alabama church bombing: four Black girls killed.

September 16:
1848: Slavery abolished in all French territories. 1949: Death of Hallie Q. Brown: Educator and lecturer for women and civil rights.

September 17:
1879: Birth of Abe "Rube" Foster: Black Baseball great. 1983: Vanessa Williams first Black crowned "Miss America". Sept. 18: 1865: Equal Rights Mass meeting held in Richmond, Virginia.

September 18:
1895: Booker T. Washington delivers his famous Atlanta Exposition speech.

September 19:
1947: Jackie Robinson: The first Black Named Baseballs: "Rookie of the Year".

September 20:
1830: First Negro National Convention was held. *Where was it held? 2008: Sebrina Philpart-Brunson performed as a line judge in the Stillman College vs. Tuskegee University, making her way as the first woman to officiate a NCAA Division II, Southern Intercollegiate Athletic Conference's (SIAC) college football game.

September 21:
1872: John Conyers enters Annapolis Naval Academy, in Maryland.

September 22:
1950: Ralph J. Bunche awarded the Nobel Peace Prize. *Why did he receive the award?

September 23:
1961: Thurgood Marshall nominated to U.S. Circuit Court of Appeals (AφA).

September 24:
1894: Birth of E. Franklin Frazier: Educator and speaker against racial prejudice.
1923: Death of Nancy "Aunt Jemima" Green: The world's first living trademark for the famous pancake mix.

September 25:
1974: Barbara Hancock: the first Black female White House Fellow.

September 26:
1937: Death of Bessie Smith: "Queen of the Blues".

September 27:
1912: W.C. Handy published "Memphis Blues". 1935: James Weldon Johnson lectured at New York University.

September 28:
1895: National Baptist Convention organized in Atlanta, Ga. 1961: Rubie Dee opened in the play "Purlie Victorious".

September 29:
1977: Mohammed Ali defeated Earnie Shavers.

September 30:
1864: 13 Blacks received the Congressional Medal of Honor. *Who were the Blacks that received the honor? 1975: Virgie M. Ammons patented the Fireplace Damper Actuating Tool.

OCTOBER

Muhammad Ali

Originally known as Cassius Clay, at the age of 22 he won the world heavyweight championship from Sonny Liston. Ali changed his name after joining the Nation of Islam in 1964, subsequently converting to Sunni Islam in 1975. In 1967, three years after Ali had won the heavyweight championship; he was publicly vilified for his refusal to be conscripted into the U.S. military, based on his religious beliefs and opposition to the Vietnam War. Ali was eventually arrested and found guilty on draft evasion charges; he was stripped of his boxing title, and his boxing license was suspended. He was not imprisoned, but did not fight again for nearly four years while his appeal worked its way up to the U.S. Supreme Court, where it was eventually successful.

Ali would go on to become the first and only three-time lineal World Heavyweight Champion.

October

October 1:
1841: Birth of Fannie M. Richards: Detroit's first Black school teacher and founder of the Phyllis Wheatley Home for Aged Black Women. 1917: J. Scott appointed Special Asst. Sec. of War.

October 2:
1863: Alexander T. Augusta: one of the first Black doctors during the Civil War.

October 3:
1974: Vernon E. Jordan named to the Clemency Board by President Ford. 1989: Art Shell (AφA): Named the first Black Head Coach of the Los Angeles Raiders.

October 4:
1864: New Orleans Tribune, "Negro Daily", began publication.

October 5:
2005: The Association for the Study of African American Life & History Inc. (ASALH). Held its 90th Annual Convention in the city of Buffalo, N.Y. under the theme: "The Niagara Movement".
2007: Marion Jones admits to steroid use in Federal court and is later stripped of her (5), 2000 Olympic medals.

October 6:
1871: Fisk University Jubilee Singers began its first national tour. 1895: W. D. Davis patented several riding saddles.

October 7:
1897: Birth of Elijah Mohammed, Black Muslims leader, Sandersville, Ga.

October 8:
1804: Jean Jacques I: Proclaimed Emperor of Haiti.

October 9:
1869: Morgan State College opened

October 10:
1984: Bishop Desmond Tutu awarded The Noble Peace Prize.

October 11:
1882: Birth of R. Nathaniel Dett: Musical composer.

October 12:
1975: Frank Robinson named the first Black Major League Baseball manager. *What baseball team did he manage?

October 13:
1837: Henry E. Hayne first Black accepted at the University of South Carolina.

October 14:
1964 Rev. Martin L. King Jr. (AΦA): Awarded the Noble Peace Prize. <u>1963: Birth of my sisters (W.A. Price) Paulette & Colette Price.</u> 1974: LeRoy T. Walker named the first Black Olympic coach. *What sport did he coach?

October 15:
1972: Jackie Robinson (AΦA) honored at Cincinnati Stadium for his baseball accomplishments. 1995: Death of Paulette T. Price (R.I.P. little sister).

October 16:
1859: John Browns raid on Harper's Ferry, W. Va. 1931: Death of William H. Crogman: Noted Classical scholar.

October 17:
1787: Blacks petitioned Massachusetts for equal educational facilities. 1888: Capital Savings Bank: The first Black operated bank opened in Washington, D.C.

October 18:
1945: Paul Robeson (AΦA) Awarded the N.A.A.C.P. Spingarn Medal. 1977: Reggie Jackson: Hit 3 home runs for New York in the World Series.

October 19:
1943: The play: "Othello" opened with Paul Robeson (AΦA) in the title role. * Where did the play open?

October 20:
1946: W.E.B. DuBois (AΦA) gave the "Behold the Lord" speech. *Where did he give this speech?

October 21:
1850: The city of Chicago, IL. refused to enforce the Fugitive Slave Act. 1872: John H. Conyers: first Black admitted to U.S. Naval Academy.

October 22:
1952: Frank E. Peterson Jr. commissioned as Marine Aviation Officer.

October 23:
1947: N.A.A.C.P. petitioned U.N. on racial injustices.

October 24:
1972: Death of Jackie Robinson.

October 25:
1806: Death of Benjamin Banneker: Famous inventor. *Can you name some of his inventions? 1940: Benjamin O. Smith Sr. promoted to Brigadier General. 1959: Birth of Judge Lynn C. Toler (in Columbus, Ohio) the arbitrator on the court series *Divorce Court*.

October 26:
1911: Birth of Mahalia Jackson, famous gospel singer in New Orleans, La.

October 27:
1821: First time a New York paper advertised a Negro stage play. *What newspaper published this performance? 1941: Death of Ernest Everett Just: The biologist who pioneered the investigation of egg fertilization.

October 28:
1972: Jackie Robinson (ΑΦΑ) biography published. *Who published his biography?

October 29:
1954: The end of segregation of races in the U.S. Armed Forces. 1973: Birth of Vonetta Jeffrey-Flowers, First African American Winter Olympic (2002) Gold medal winner (Two Woman Bobsleigh).

October 30:
1945: Booker T. Washington entered the Hall of Fame for Great Americans.

October 31:
1974: Mohammed Ali vs. George Foreman for the Heavy Weight Championship. *Where did the fight take place? What was the outcome of the fight?

NOVEMBER

Rotimi Adebari

Rotimi Adebari (born 1964 in Okeodan, Ogun State) is a Nigerian-born Irish politician. He was elected as the **first black mayor in Ireland**. A convert from Islam to Christianity, he fled Nigeria in 2000, and made a claim for asylum on the grounds of religious persecution. His application was rejected because of insufficient evidence he had personally suffered persecution, but he gained residency because his third child, another boy, was born in Ireland. Against claims that he was a train operator working out of the Queens Park depot on the Bakerloo tube line, Adebari says he travelled to Ireland directly from Nigeria, via Paris, and never worked or lived in London at any time. He and his family settled in County Laois. In 2004, he was elected as a town councilor in local elections. In June 2007 he was elected as mayor of Portlaoise Town Council (9 members), with support from Fine Gael, Sinn Féin and an Independent councilor. In the 2009 local elections he was re-elected to the town council and also to Laois County Council for the Portlaoise electoral area. He completed his master's degree in intercultural studies at Dublin City University. And set up a firm called Optimum Point Consultancy. He ran as an Independent candidate in the 2011 general election for the Laois–Offaly constituency, though failed to get elected. He received 628 1st preference votes, a share of 0.85%. He is also a regular presenter on Midlands 103.

NOVEMBER

November 1:
1787: The first state school for free Blacks opened in New York City. 1866: The first Civil Rights Bill was passed.

November 2:
1903: St. Luke Penny Savings Bank opened and founded by Maggie L. Walker. *Where was the bank located?

November 3:
1974: Harold Ford elected Congressman for Tennessee. 1976: Death of Charles D. Dixon, the first Black to conduct a major symphony orchestra.

November 4:
1953: Hulan Jack elected the borough President of Manhattan, N.Y. 2008: Barack Obama became the first Black elected President of the United States of America. *What was the electoral vote count for this famous win?

November 5:
1974: Black Caucus rose to 17. *What was the previous number and why was it raised?

November 6:
1919: Supreme Court upheld housing rights in Louisville, Kentucky. 1973: Coleman Young (Detroit) and Tom Bradley (Los Angeles) became the first Black mayors of cities with populations greater than one million people.

November 7:
1955: The U.S. Supreme Court banned Segregation in recreational facilities.

November 8:
1966: Edward Brooks elected First Black Senator since Reconstruction. *What state was he elected?

November 9:
1868: Howard University Medical School opened. 2006: Death of Edward Bradley. He was the first African American White House correspondent and a "60 Minutes" Journalist for 25 years. He received over 19 Emmys and awards for his journalism excellence.

November 10:
1960: Andrew Hatcher named Associate Press Secretary to President Kennedy. 2006: Death of R & B singer, Gerald Levertt.

November 11:
1989: Civil Rights Memorial dedicated in Montgomery, Al.

November 12:
1922: Sigma Gamma Rho Sorority was founded at Butler University.

November 13:
1839: First anti-slavery political party (Liberty Party) organized. 2006: The groundbreaking for the Martin L. King Jr. monument took place in Washington, DC.

November 14:
1950: Lydia Holmes patented several wood toys. 1954: Birth of Condoleezza Rice, first African American woman to be appointed National Security Advisor. 1977: Trial began for the 1963 Birmingham church bombing case. *What was the name of the Church? 2007: Nigerian-born Rotimi Adebari made history when he was elected the first Black Mayor (in the Republic of Ireland) of Portlaoise (Port-leash-a), Ireland.

November 15:
218 B.C.: Hannibal, full-blooded Black man, crossed the Alps.

November 16:
1873: Birth of W.C. Handy, "Father of the Blues". 1892: Behanzin defended his native land, Dahomey, W. Africa against France.

November 17:
1636: Henrique Dias, an ex-slave led and won a battle against the Dutch. *Where did the battle take place? 1911: Omega Psi Phi Fraternity was founded at Howard University.

November 18:
1787: Birth of Sojourner Truth in New York. *Why is she important to Black history?

November 19:
1911: Omega Psi Phi Fraternity was founded at Howard University. 1953: Roy Campanella named "Most Valuable Player" (M.V.P.) in National Baseball League.

November 20:
1962: Discrimination was banned in **All** Federally Aided Housing.

November 21:
1865: Shaw University, founded in North Carolina. 1933: S. H. Love patented an improved Vending Machine.

November 22:
1930: Elijah Mohammed founded the Nation of Islam in Detroit. 1948: Levi Jackson elected the first Black captain for the Yale football team.

November 23:
1897: Death of A.J. Beard: inventor of the Automatic Railroad Car ("Jenny Coupler") Coupler. 1897: J. L. Love patented the Pencil Sharpener. 1980: National Black Independent Party formed.

November 24:
1957: Jim Brown of the Cleveland Browns set the N.F.L. record for yards gained.

November 25:
1955: I.C.C. banned segregation in interstate travel.

November 26:
1883: Death of Sojourner Truth. 1962: Birth of Darren Arbet, first African American Arena Football League head coach to win Arena Bowl (Team: San Jose Saber Cats)

November 27:
1990: Charles Johnson awarded the National Book Award for fiction book, "Middle Passage".

November 28:
1960: Novelist Richard Wright dies.

November 29:
1905: Chicago "Defender" began publication. 1908: Birth of Adam Clayton Powell Jr. (ΑΦΑ): Congressman and Minister.

November 30:
1897: J.A. Sweeting patented the cigarette roller.

DECEMBER

Kwanzaa Celebration **Maulana Karenga**

Kwanzaa is a week-long celebration held in the United States and also celebrated in the Western African Diaspora in other nations of the Americas. The celebration honors African heritage in African-American culture, and is observed from December 26 to January 1, culminating in a feast and gift-giving. Kwanzaa has seven core principles (*Nguzo Saba*): Unity, self-determination, collective work and responsibility, cooperative economics, purpose, creativity, and faith. It was created by Maulana Karenga, and was first celebrated in 1966–67.

DECEMBER

December 1:
1955: Rosa Parks' refusal to take a back seat on a segregated bus starts the Montgomery Bus Boycott.

December 2:
1859: John Brown, abolitionist was executed for insurrection. *1884: Granville Woods invented a telephone which was much better than the one created by Alexander Graham Bell. What other items did he invent? 1969: Marie V. Brittan-Brown patented the Security System.

December 3:
1847: Frederick Douglass (AΦA). Published the first issue of the "North Star" newspaper.

December 4:
1906: Alpha Phi Alpha (AΦA) Fraternity founded as the first Black collegiate Greek Letter Fraternity at Cornell University, Ithaca, N.Y. 2006: 100th Anniversary of Alpha Phi Alpha Fraternity Inc. (AΦA)

December 5:
1784: Death of Phyllis Wheatley, Black poet. 1935: National Council of Negro Woman was founded, New York. 2008: Turner Gill made history by taking the University of Buffalo (7-5) football team to its first MAC League Championship and defeated Ball State (12-0) 42 to 24.

December 6:
1890: Sgt. Thomas Shaw earned the Congressional Medal of Honor.

December 7:
1896: Antonio Maceo died a martyr for the "Liberty" of Cuba. 1947: Birth of Bishop Wilton Daniel Gregory, first African American President of the United States Conference of Catholic Bishops.

December 8:
1896: J.T. White patented an improvement to the lemon squeezer.

December 9:
1946: Committee on Civil Rights organized by Executive Order.

December 10:
1846: Norbert Rillieux patented sugar-making equipment. 1984: Bishop Desmond Tutu received the Nobel Peace Prize.

December 11:
1872: P.B.S. Pinchback became the Acting Governor of Louisiana.

December 12:
1899: G. F. Grant patented the Golf Tee. 1950: Jesse Leroy Brown becomes the first African American naval officer to die in combat.

December 13:
1973: Bro. David Dinkins (ΑΦΑ) named Deputy Mayor of New York City.

December 14:
*1939: Birth of Ernie J. Davis: The first Black to win the "Heisman Trophy". *What college did he attend? 1973: Fourteen Black college Presidents met with President Nixon regarding funding for Black colleges.

December 15:
1791: The Bill of Rights took effect.

December 16:
1976: Bro. Andrew Young (ΑΦΑ) appointed Ambassador to the United Nations.

December 17:
1973: Georgia State Representative Julian Bond promoted to Health Care Legislation committee.

December 18:
1865: 13th Amendment ratified. *What was the 13th Amendment?

December 19:
1875: Birth of Carter G. Woodson "Father of Black History".

December 20:
1933: J. Jackson published the book "Am I A Soldier of the Cross".

December 21:
1920: W. H. Sammons patented hair-straightening comb. 1956: Montgomery, Al. buses became integrated.

December 22:
1941: Atlanta Urban League won the battle for the use of "Mrs." for Black women.

December 23:
1869: Madam C. J. Walker, a businesswoman and first African American woman millionaire was born. 1975: Stanley Scott appointed to the A.I.D. African Staff.

December 24:
1814: Black troops held position, in Battle of New Orleans. 1832: A charter was granted to the Georgia Infirmary. The first Black Georgia hospital located was located in Savannah, Ga.

December 25: <u>CHRISTMAS DAY</u>.
1760: Jupiter Hammon a Black slave published: "Salvation of Christ". 2006: Death of James Brown "Godfather of Soul". He was also known as the "Hardest Working Man in Show Business".

December 26: <u>Beginning of Boxing Day (Canada) & KWANZAA:</u>
A non-religious African American holiday created by Dr. Maulana Karenga, which celebrates family, community and culture. It is celebrated for seven days: December 26 – January 1. 1908: Jack Johnson became the first, Black Heavyweight boxing champion.

December 27:
1887: Stewart & Johnson patented the metal bending machine.

December 28:
1905: Earl "Father" Hines, "Father of Modern Jazz Piano" was born.

December 29:
Death: Kelly Miller: First Black admitted to Hopkins University. 1746: Lucy Terry, poet, wrote her first poem. * Do you know the name of the poem?

December 30:
1800: African-Americans made up 20% of the U.S. population. * What was the African American population at that time? What is it now?

December 31:
1952: The first full year in 71 years without a reported lynching in the U.S. 1995: Birthday of Gabrielle Douglas: Became the first American to win the "All Around" Gymnastics event in the 2012 Summer Olympics, in England.

"History is Not What Makes You. You are What Makes History"
Willie A. Price

Gabrielle Douglas was introduced to gymnastics by way of a cartwheel. Her older sister, Arielle – a former gymnast and competitive cheerleader, was determined to teach the toddler the sport she loved. Gabrielle immediately picked up her older sister's love of the sport and soon taught herself how to do a one armed cartwheel.

After two years of poking and prodding, Arielle convinced their mother, Natalie, to allow Gabrielle to train at a local gym. Once formal training began, another two years was all it took for Virginia to crown Gabrielle as the new 2004 Gymnastics State Champion.

Gabrielle soon reached her peak at her local gym, quickly accumulating numerous victories and top finishes over the next few years. The task became clear; Gabrielle had to convince her mother to allow her, the youngest, to move across the country in pursuit of her Olympic dream. This would allow her an opportunity to train under elite coach Liang Chow in West Des Moines, IA. At age 14, having overcome a number of obstacles placed before her, Gabrielle left Virginia Beach and her family behind to train with Liang Chow. Living with a host family, the Partons, Gabrielle now plays the role of big sister to their four girls.

Since leaving home, Gabrielle has earned a Team Gold at the 2011 World Championships, placed first at the 2012 Olympic Trials (earning the only guaranteed spot on the Olympic Team), 2012 Olympic Team Gold and the 2012 Women's Gymnastics Olympic All-Around Title. Making her not only the **first African American** to ever receive the All-Around title, but also the only female gymnasts in history to possess both Team and All-Around Gold in the same Olympics. Gabrielle also plans to compete in the 2016 Olympics in Rio de Janeiro, Brazil.

Ernestine Shepherd

Ernestine "Ernie" Shepherd, at age 75, is a personal trainer, a professional model, a competitive bodybuilder and happier and more fulfilled than she's ever been in her life. In March of 2010, on stage in Rome, Italy she was formally given the title of World's Oldest Performing Female Body Builder (by Guinness World Records). How did Ernestine transform herself from an average middle-aged woman to bodybuilding diva?

The 5-foot-5, 130-pound dynamo wakes up at 3 a.m. every morning, and runs 10 miles a day, before hitting the gym for pushups, pull-ups and a heavy regimen of free weights, all to the amazement of her 80 year old husband of 54 years, her 53-year-old son, and her 14-year-old grandson.

"From Kings to Presidents"
(2006 – Present)

- 1) EL HADJ SEIDOU NJIMOLUH NJOYA (CAMEROON)
  Sultan of Fumban and Mfon of the Bamun
- 2) OSEADEEYO ADDO DANKWA III (GHANA)
  King of Apkropong-Akuapem
- 3) SALOMON IGBINOGHODUA (NIGERIA)
  Oba Erediauwa of Be'nin
- 4) ABUBAKAR SIDIQ (NIGERIA)
  Sultan of Sokoto
- 5) HAPI IV (CAMEROON)
  King of Bana
- 6) HALIDOU SALI (CAMEROON)
  Lamido of Bibemi
- 7) GOODWILL ZWELETHINI (SOUTH AFRICA)
  King of Zulu
- 8) ALIYU MUSTAPHA (NIGERIA)
  Lamido of Adamawa
- 9) BOUBA ABDOULAYE (CAMEROON)
  Sultan of Rey-Bouba
- 10) HADJ MAMADOU KABIR USMAN (NIGERIA)
  Emir of Katsina
- 11) AGBOLI-AGBO DEDJLANI (BENIN)
  King of Abomey
- 12) JOSEPH LANGANFIN (BENIN)

- 13) IGWE KENNETH NNAJI ONYEMAEKE ORIZU III (NIGERIA)
  Obi of Nnewi
- 14) ISIENWENRO JAMES IYOHA INNEH (NIGERIA)
  Ekegbian of Be'nin
- 15) NYIMI KOK MABIINTSH III
  King of Kuba
- 16) OBA JOSEPH ADEKOLA OGUNOYE
  Olowo of Owo
- 17) NELSON MANDELLA (SOUTH AFRICA)
  The First Black President of South Africa
- 18) BARACK OBAMA (UNITED STATES OF AMERICA)
  The First Black President of the United States of America

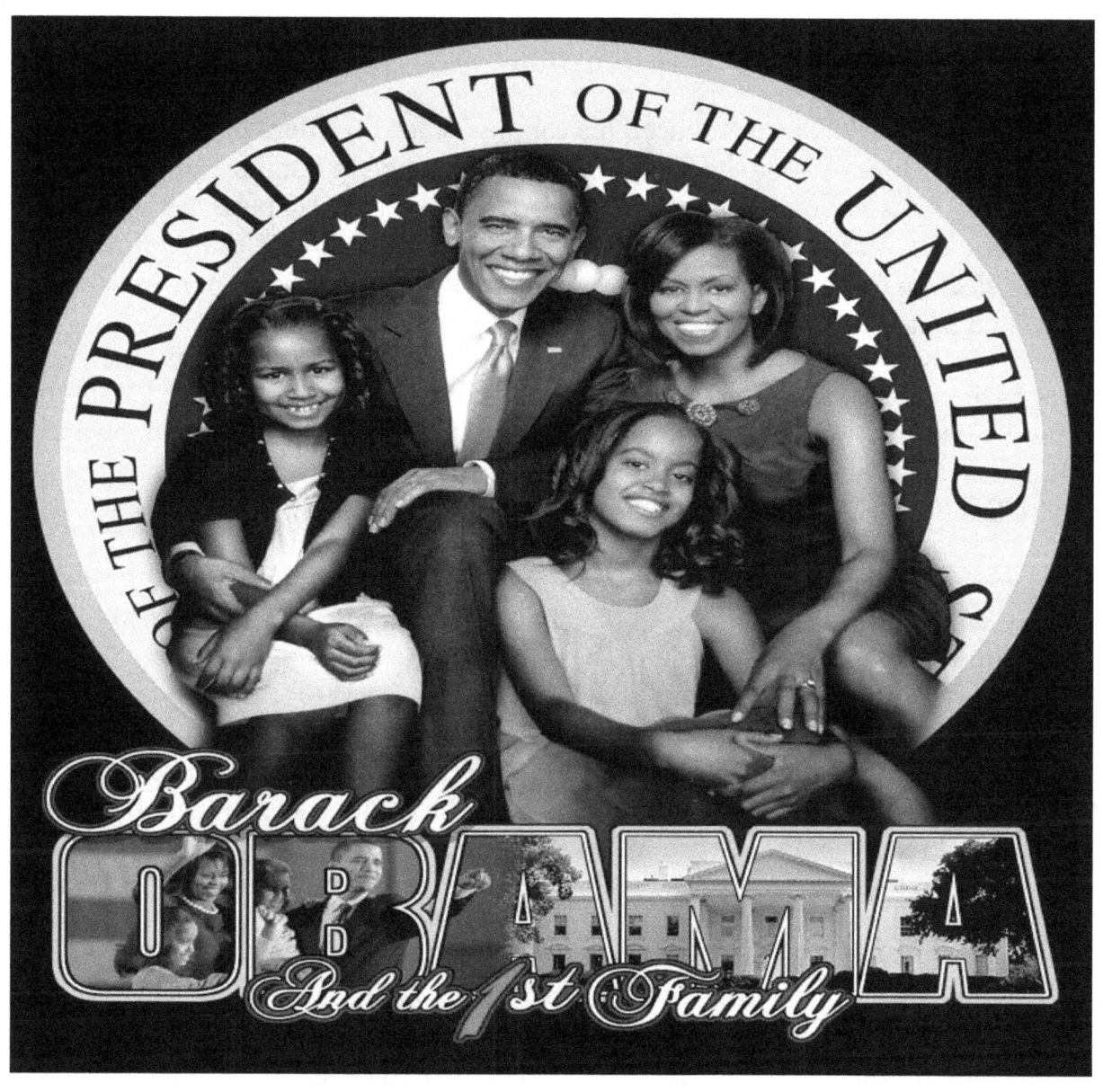

Barack Hussein Obama II (born August 4, 1961) is the President-elect of the United States and the junior United States Senator from Illinois. Obama is the first African American to be elected President of the United States.

He is a graduate of Columbia College of Columbia University and Harvard Law School, where he was president of the Harvard Law Review. Obama worked as a community organizer and practiced as a civil rights attorney before serving three terms in the Illinois Senate from 1997 to 2004. He taught constitutional law at the University of Chicago Law School from 1992 to 2004. Following an unsuccessful bid for a seat in the U.S. House of Representatives in 2000, he announced his campaign for the U.S. Senate in January 2003, won a primary victory in March 2004, and was elected to the Senate in November 2004. Obama delivered the keynote address at the Democratic National Convention in July 2004.

On February 10, 2007, he announced his candidacy for President of the United States, and on June 3, 2008, he was named the presumptive nominee of the Democratic Party after a 17-month-long primary campaign. He became the President-elect after defeating Republican presidential candidate John McCain in the general election on November 4, 2008, with and is due to be sworn in as President of the United States on January 20, 2009.

Barack Obama was born at the Kapi'olani Medical Center for Women & Children in Honolulu, Hawaii, to Barack Obama, Sr., a Luo from Nyang'oma Kogelo, Nyanza Province, Kenya, and Ann Dunham, a white American from Wichita, Kansas of mainly English, Irish and smaller amounts of German descent.

As an adult Obama admitted that during high school he used marijuana, cocaine and alcohol, which he described at the 2008 Civil Forum on the Presidency as his greatest moral failure.

Following high school, Obama moved to Los Angeles, where he studied at Occidental College for two years. He then transferred to Columbia University in New York City, where he majored in political science with a specialization in international relations. Obama graduated with a B.A. from Columbia in 1983, then at the start of the following year worked for a year at the Business International Corporation and then at the New York Public Interest Research Group.

After four years in New York City, Obama moved to Chicago, where he was hired as director of the Developing Communities Project (DCP), a church-based community organization originally comprising eight Catholic parishes in Greater Roseland (Roseland, West Pullman, and Riverdale) on Chicago's far South Side, and worked there for three years from June 1985 to May 1988. During his three years as the DCP's director, its staff grew from one to thirteen and its annual budget grew from $70,000 to $400,000, with accomplishments including helping set up a job training program, a college preparatory tutoring program, and a tenants' rights organization in Altgeld Gardens.

Obama entered Harvard Law School in late 1988. At the end of his first year, he was selected, based on his grades and a writing competition, as an editor of the Harvard Law Review. In February 1990, in his second year, he was elected president of the Law Review, a full-time volunteer position functioning as editor-in-chief and supervising the Law Review's staff of eighty editors. Obama's election as the first black president of the Law Review was widely reported and followed by several long, detailed profiles. During his summers, he returned to Chicago where he worked as a summer associate at the law firms of Sidley & Austin in 1989 and Hopkins & Sutter in 1990. After graduating with a Juris Doctor (J.D.) magna cum laude from Harvard in 1991, he returned to Chicago.

The publicity from his election as the first black president of the Harvard Law Review led to a publishing contract and advance for a book about race relations. In an effort to recruit him to their faculty, the University of Chicago Law School provided Obama with a fellowship and an office to work on his book He originally planned to finish the book in one year, but it took much longer as the book evolved into a personal memoir. In order to work without interruptions, Obama and his wife, Michelle, traveled to Bali where he wrote for several months. The manuscript was finally published in mid-1995 as Dreams from My Father.

Obama directed Illinois' Project Vote from April to October 1992, a voter registration drive with a staff of ten and seven hundred volunteers; it achieved its goal of registering 150,000 of 400,000 unregistered African Americans in the state, and led to Crain's Chicago Business naming Obama to its 1993 list of "40 under Forty" powers to be.

Obama taught constitutional law at the University of Chicago Law School for twelve years, being first classified as a Lecturer from 1992 to 1996, and then as a Senior Lecturer from 1996 to 2004. He also joined Davis, Miner, Barnhill & Galland, a twelve-attorney law firm specializing in civil rights litigation and neighborhood economic development, where he was an associate for three years from 1993 to 1996, then of counsel from 1996 to 2004, with his law license becoming inactive in 2002.

Obama was a founding member of the board of directors of Public Allies in 1992, resigning before his wife, Michelle, became the founding executive director of Public Allies Chicago in early 1993. He served from 1994 to 2002 on the board of directors of the Woods Fund of Chicago, which in 1985 had been the first foundation to fund the Developing Communities Project, and also from 1994 to 2002 on the board of directors of The Joyce Foundation. Obama served on the board of directors of the Chicago Annenberg Challenge from 1995 to 2002, as founding president and chairman of the board of directors from 1995 to 1999. He also served on the board of directors of the Chicago Lawyers' Committee for Civil Rights Under Law, the Center for Neighborhood Technology, and the Lugenia Burns Hope Center.[18]

State legislator, 1997–2004

      Main article: Illinois Senate career of Barack Obama

Obama was elected to the Illinois Senate in 1996, succeeding State Senator Alice Palmer as Senator from Illinois' 13th District, which then spanned Chicago South Side neighborhoods from Hyde Park-Kenwood south to South Shore and west to Chicago Lawn. Once elected, Obama gained bipartisan support for legislation reforming ethics and health care laws. He sponsored a law increasing tax credits for low-income workers, negotiated welfare reform, and promoted increased subsidies for childcare. In 2001, as co-chairman of the bipartisan Joint Committee on Administrative Rules, Obama supported Republican Governor Ryan's payday loan regulations and predatory mortgage lending regulations aimed at averting home foreclosures.

Obama was reelected to the Illinois Senate in 1998, and again in 2002. In 2000, he lost a Democratic primary run for the U.S. House of Representatives to four-term incumbent Bobby Rush by a margin of two to one.

In mid-2002, Obama began considering a run for the U.S. Senate; he enlisted political strategist David Axelrod that fall and formally announced his candidacy in January 2003. Decisions by Republican incumbent Peter Fitzgerald and his Democratic predecessor Carol Moseley Braun not to contest the race launched wide-open Democratic and Republican primary contests involving fifteen candidates. Obama's candidacy was boosted by Axelrod's advertising campaign featuring images of the late Chicago Mayor Harold Washington and an endorsement by the daughter of the late Paul Simon, former U.S. Senator for Illinois. He received over 52% of the vote in the March 2004 primary, emerging 29% ahead of his nearest Democratic rival.

In July 2004, Obama wrote and delivered the keynote address at the 2004 Democratic National Convention in Boston, Massachusetts

Obama's expected opponent in the general election, Republican primary winner Jack Ryan, withdrew from the race in June 2004. Two months later and less than three months before Election Day, Alan Keyes accepted the Illinois Republican Party's nomination to replace Ryan. A long-time resident of Maryland, Keyes established legal residency in Illinois with the nomination. In the November 2004 general election, Obama received 70% of the vote to Keyes's 27%, the largest victory margin for a statewide race in Illinois history.

Obama was sworn in as a senator on January 4, 2005. Obama was the fifth African-American Senator in U.S. history, and the third to have been popularly elected. He is the only Senate member of the Congressional Black Caucus. CQ Weekly, a nonpartisan publication, characterized him as a "loyal Democrat" based on analysis of all Senate votes in 2005–2007, and the National Journal ranked him as the "most liberal" senator based on an assessment of selected votes during 2007. In 2005 he was ranked sixteenth, and in 2006 he was ranked tenth. In 2008, Congress.org ranked him as the eleventh most powerful Senator.

On February 10, 2007, Obama announced his candidacy for President of the United States in front of the Old State Capitol building in Springfield, Illinois. The choice of the announcement site was symbolic because it was also where Abraham Lincoln delivered his historic "House Divided" speech in 1858. Throughout the campaign, Obama emphasized the issues of rapidly ending the Iraq War, increasing energy independence, and providing universal health care, at one point identifying these as his top three priorities.

Obama on stage with his wife and two daughters just before announcing his presidential campaign in Springfield, Illinois

In March 2008, a controversy broke out concerning Obama's former pastor of twenty years, Jeremiah Wright, after ABC News broadcast clips of his racially and politically charged sermons. Initially, Obama responded by defending Wright's wider role in Chicago's African-American community, but condemned his remarks and ended Wright's relationship with the campaign. During the controversy, Obama delivered a speech entitled "A More Perfect Union" that addressed issues of race. Obama subsequently resigned from Trinity United Church of Christ "to avoid the impression that he endorsed the entire range of opinions expressed at that church."

On June 19, Obama became the first major-party presidential candidate to turn down public financing in the general election since the system was created in 1976, reversing his earlier intention to accept it.
On August 23, 2008, Obama selected Delaware Senator Joe Biden as his vice presidential running mate. At the Democratic National Convention in Denver, Colorado, Obama's former rival Hillary Clinton gave a speech strongly supporting Obama's candidacy and later called for Obama to be nominated by acclamation as the Democratic presidential candidate. Then, on August 28, Obama delivered a speech to the 84,000 supporters in Denver. During the speech, which was viewed by over 38 million people worldwide, he accepted his party's nomination and presented his policy goals.
On November 2, 2008, Obama's grandmother, Madelyn Dunham, died from cancer at the age of 86. Obama learned of his grandmother's death on November 3, one day before the election.

Obama's election sparked spontaneous street celebrations in the United States and abroad. Many editorialized that the image of the United States abroad that was strained during the administration of George Bush would improve. Fears that gun laws would become more restrictive during an Obama administration led to an unprecedented rise in firearms sales across the United States.

On November 4, 2008, Barack Obama defeated John McCain and became the first African American to be elected President of the United States. In his victory speech, delivered before a crowd of hundreds of thousands of his supporters in Grant Park in Chicago, Obama proclaimed that "change has come to America." Born in Hawaii, Obama will be the first U.S. President born outside the contiguous United States. He also will be fifth youngest President at a date of accession and the second since Lincoln whose primary political base is Illinois.

President-elect Obama was sworn in as the 44th President of the United States on January 20, 2009. On November 6, 2012, he won re-election for a second term as President of the United States against Mitt Romney.

Obama met his wife, Michelle Robinson, in June 1989 when he was employed as a summer associate at the Chicago law firm of Sidley Austin. Assigned for three months as Obama's adviser at the firm, Robinson joined him at group social functions, but declined his initial offers to date. They began dating later that summer, became engaged in 1991, and were married on October 3, 1992. The couple's first daughter, Malia Ann, was born in 1998, followed by a second daughter, Natasha ("Sasha"), in 2001.

Main article: Public image of Barack Obama

With his Kenyan father and white American mother, his upbringing in Honolulu and Jakarta, and his Ivy League education, Obama's early life experiences differ markedly from those of African-American politicians who launched their careers in the 1960s through participation in the civil rights movement. Expressing puzzlement over questions about whether he is "black enough," Obama told an August 2007 meeting of the National Association of Black Journalists that the debate is not about his physical appearance or his record on issues of concern to black voters. Obama said that "we're still locked in this notion that if you appeal to white folks then there must be something wrong."

Echoing the inaugural address of John F. Kennedy, Obama acknowledged his youthful image in an October 2007 campaign speech, saying: "I wouldn't be here if, time and again, the torch had not been passed to a new generation." A popular catch phrase distilled the concept: ***"Rosa sat so Martin could walk; Martin walked so Obama could run."***

The Obama Family

MY INVENTION
(Level I)

You can see the inventor and the invention. But, can you spell the invention? The purpose of this game is to show these Black inventions and to encourage the student to learn the proper spelling of those inventions.

AFRICANS   _____

G. E. BECKET   _____

JOHN A. BURR   _____

BURRIDGE & MARCHMAN   _____

T. ELKINS   _____

ROBERT FLEMING JR.   _____

AUGUSTUS JACKSON   _____

W. A. MARTIN   _____

GRANVILLE T. WOODS   _____

Copyright © Willie A. Price 2008

Find The Black Inventions (level1)

```
M R B U G G Y I
P A U O U I E A
M E I I R H B T
A H T L L E N O
L A V A B L P I
R Y S M D O Q L
L S H O E C X E
M H E S W K Q T
```

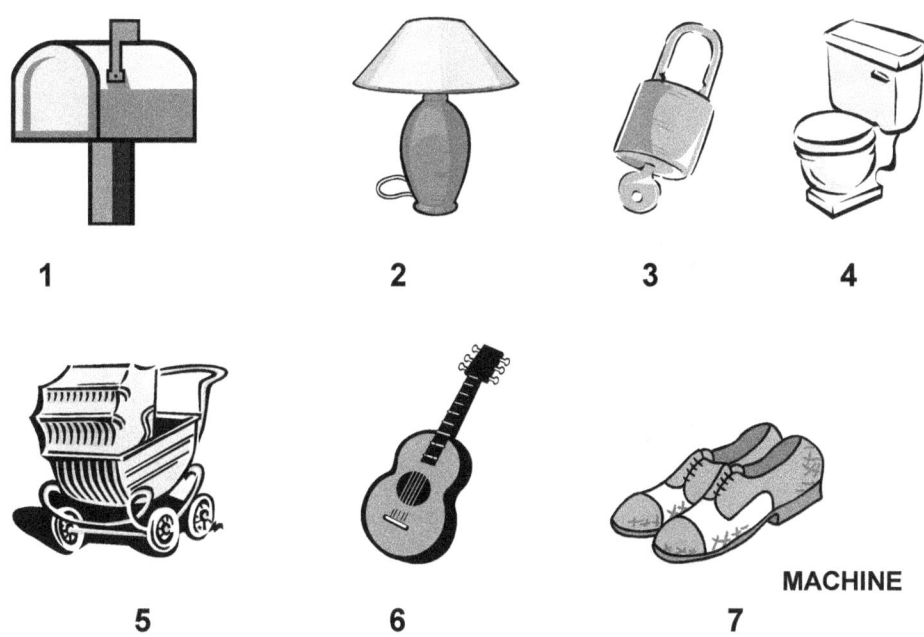

1
2
3
4
5
6
7 MACHINE

African / Black Inventions (Level 1)

| 1 across | 3 across | 5 Across | 9 across | 10 across | 11 across |

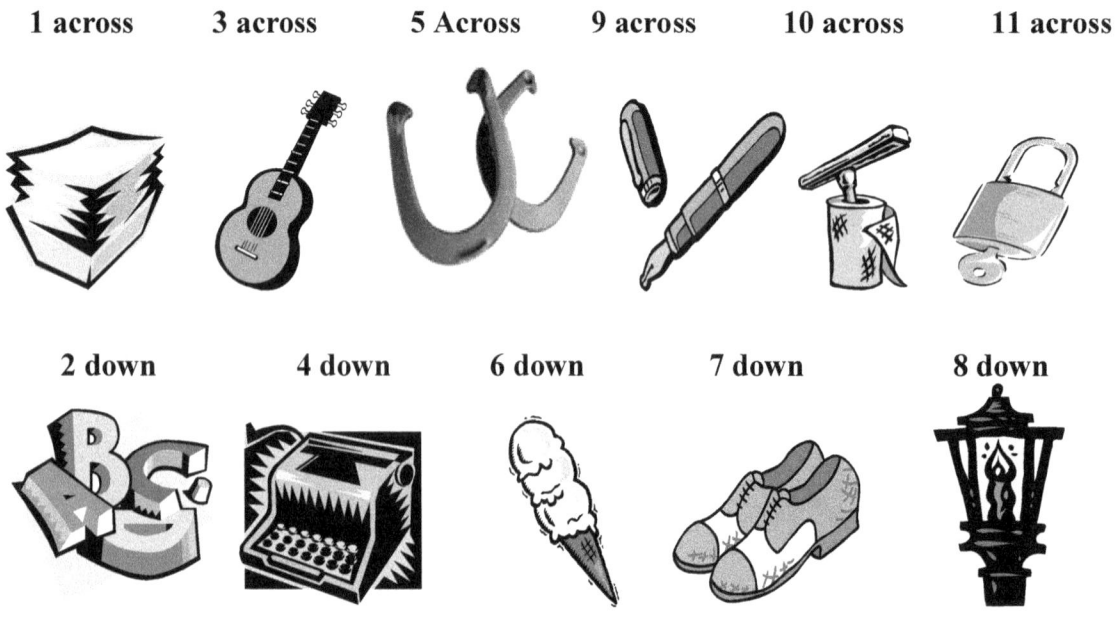

| 2 down | 4 down | 6 down | 7 down | 8 down |

Copyright © Willie A. Price 2008

Black Inventions Word Scramble (level 1)

1. P M O
2. E S O H
3. C L O K
4. P R E A P
5. O R O D   N O B K
6. L G O F   E T E
7. H S C E S   A E S M G
8. O L T E I T
9. R T U G I A
10. E I C   R A C E M

1) _____
2) _____
3) _____
4) _____
5) _____
6) _____
7) _____
8) _____
9) _____
10) _____

Black Inventions Word Scramble (Level 2)

1. L H B T E A P A
2. I Y L B C C E   R M E A F
3. E L L R C L U A   H N P O E
4. H S C E S   A E S M G
5. O R O D   N O B K
6. R O D O   O P S T
7. G E G   B A E E T R
8. V T R O A E L E
9. L G O F   E T E
10. R T U G I A
11. R T O I E E P C L H
12. E I C   R A C E M
13. N E N L A T R
14. L N W A   E O R W M
15. C L O K
16. N C D M E I I E
17. U E R P S   R K O E A S   N G E A U R T W
18. O L T E I T
19. R T R E Y T P W I E
20. S U D T   A N P
21. O S S O E H E R H
22. P M O
23. P R E A P
24. E S O H
25. W E C R N H

Copyright © Willie A. Price 2008

"Follow the Leader"
(Level 2)

The following are personalities who have been the first. All of the answers can be located in this book.

The First Black Mayor of the City of Buffalo, NY

She was the first Black woman appointed as a Federal Judge.

He was the first Black lawyer to practice before the U. S. Supreme Court.

They were the first Black head coaches to bring opposing teams to a Super Bowl.

He was the first Black killed during the "American Revolution".

He became the first Black officer in the U. S. Navy.

She was the first woman (Black or White) to be nominated to the post of Chairperson for the Nuclear Regulations Commission.

He was the first Black cowboy admitted to the National Rodeo Hall of Fame.

He was the first Black man to win an Oscar Award.

She was the first Black woman admitted to the Bar.

He was the first Black man admitted to the New York State Bar Association.

She was the first Black woman to drive a United States mail coach.

He was the first Black millionaire in America.

She was the first Black woman millionaire in America.

He was the first Black admitted to the West Point Academy.

He was the first Black man to receive a Doctor of Divinity degree.

He was the first Black lawyer admitted to the Florida Bar Association and the author of the Black National Anthem.

He was the first President of the Black Labor Union.

He performed the world's first successful open heart surgery.

Copyright © Willie A. Price 2008

Contemporary Black Inventors
(Level 2)

The goal of this game is to match the inventor with the invention and the inventions date and year. All of the information can be found in this Black History book.

Inventor	Invention	Invention Date
1) A. P. ABOURNE	GUITAR	OCTOBER 6, 1895
2) FREDERICK JONES	LAWN SPRINKLER	MARCH 3, 1886
3) ALFRED L. CRALLE	AIR CONDITION	NOVEMBER 21, 1933
4) LYDIA HOLMES	FOUNTAIN PEN	JULY 12, 1949
5) G. F. GRANT	SECURITY SYSTEM	JANUARY 7, 1890
6) HENRY SAMPSON	GOLF TEE	DECEMBER 2, 1884
7) GRANVILLE WOODS	FIREPLACE DAMPER TOOL	JULY 27, 1980
8) J. L. LOVE	FIRE EXTINGUISHER	FEBRUARY 2, 1897
9) J. S. SMITH	ICE CREAM SCOOPER	SEPTEMBER 30, 1975
10) MARIE BRITTAN BROWN	RIDING SADDLES	MAY 4, 1897
11) ROBERT FLEMMING	CELLULAR TELEPHONE	NOVEMBER 14, 1950
12) S. H. LOVE	WOOD TOYS PATENT	DECEMBER 12, 1899
13) THOMAS J. MARTIN	PENCIL SHARPENER	JULY 6, 1971
14) VIRGIE M. AMMONS	IMPROVED TELEPHONE	NOVEMBER 23, 1897
15) W. B. PURVIS	VENDING MACHINE	MARCH 26, 1872
16) W. D. DAVIS	REFINING OF COCONUT OIL	DECEMBER 2, 1969

Copyright © Willie A. Price 2008

What's My Name?
(Level 2)

Can you match these entertainers to their real names?

Actual Name

1. CAMERON GILES
2. ROBERT S. KELLY
3. RICARDO BROWN
4. DANA ELAINE OWENS
5. WILLIE NORWOOD JR.
6. PERCY MILLER JR.
7. CORNELL HAYNES JR.
8. KIMBERLY JONES
9. JAMES TODD SMITH
10. DWAYNE JOHNSON
11. JEFFREY ATKINS
12. E. JIHAN JEFFERS
13. CHRIS BRIDGES
14. ROBYN FENTY

Entertainment Name

A. L.L. COOL J.
B. THE ROCK
C. LIL' KIM
E. LUDACRIS
F. NELLY
G. RIHANNA
H. CAM'RON
I. RAY J.
J. EVE
L. KURUPT
M. R. KELLY
N. JA RULE
O. QUEEN LATIFAH
P. LIL' ROMEO

Copyright © Willie A. Price 2008

"Riddle Me This" (Level 2)

```
P E A N U T B U T T E R
A D V A B M A H D S U H
M U M F P M S F M E F J
S O M A A E M A E W R A
B R O W N S I G N D A C
A D S A Z L T F K U M K
V W E F L B H V I R E S
M A S I P S G E N E G O
A Y W A S H I N G T O N
H N P H E O S E M I B M
A E D C R E A M H R E A
R V K A L L E N O W K H
```

1) James, Jim and Whitney's man Bobby share this name.
2) Issac hayes, Harriet Tubman, Nickname.
3) Jiffy should be forever thankful to Mr. Carver for this.
4) lock, John and Ladies Love Todd.
5) Vanessa, Serena and Venus
6) Martin, Lion, Chess piece and Regina
7) George, District not a state and Denzel.
8) Type, book, play and song
9) Coffee, Ice, Cookies and, Shaving
10) Picture, Bike and Building
11) Toilet, News, Copy and Fax
12) Peter, Dust and Frying
13) Horse, Lace, Buckle and Shine
14) Michael, Jesse, Janet and Reggie
15) Marcus, Edger----Poe and Iverson
16) East, Kanye and Wild
17) John, LiL, Bruce

Copyright © Willie A. Price 2008

Black Inventors (Level 3)

We are trying to determine which items are Black inventions. We need your help locating the inventors of the items listed below (Via internet, history books, etc.). List the inventor next to the area of the invention and the year. All of the answers can be found in this book.

Invention	Inventor	Year Invented or Patented
Chess Game	_____	_____
Folding Chair	_____	_____
Guided Missile	_____	_____
Street Sweeper	_____	_____
Blood Plasma	_____	_____
Space Shuttle Retrieval Arm	_____	_____
Programmable Remote Control	_____	_____
Super Soaker Water Gun	_____	_____
Baby Buggy	_____	_____
Clothes Drier	_____	_____
Lawn Sprinkler	_____	_____
Helicopter	_____	_____
Cellular Telephone	_____	_____

Copyright © Willie A. Price 2008

What's My Name?
(Level 3)
Can you match these entertainers to their real names?

Actual Name | **Entertainment Name**

A) KENNETH EDMONDS

B) EARL SIMMONS

C) A. AUGELLO COOK

D) TIFFANY COBB

E) JAYCEON TAYLOR

F) ELGIN LUMPKINS

G) ARTIS IVEY JR.

H) CORDOZAR BROADUS

I) O'SHEA JACKSON

J) JOHN STEPHENS

K) A. LAVERNE BROWN

L) KAREN JOHNSON

M) TREVOR SMITH

N) MARIE WRIGHT

O) DARRYL RICHARDSON II

P) LORI ANN RAMBOUGH

Q) T. DARNELL GIBSON

R) S. JUDKINS HARDAWAY

S) DWIGHT ERRINGTON MYERS

T) SHAWN COREY CARTER

1. THE GAME
2. ANGIE STONE
3. JOHN LEGEND
4. HEAVY D
5. BUSTA RHYMES
6. ICE CUBE
7. GINUWINE
8. FREE
9. JAY-Z
10. SNOOP DOGG
11. LIL SCRAPPY
12. TYRESE
13. BLU CANTRELL
14. BABYFACE
15. WHOOPI GOLDBERG
16. STEVIE WONDER
17. DMX
18. COOLIO
19. ALICIA KEYS
20. SOMMORE

Copyright © Willie A. Price 2013

"Follow the Leader"
(Level 3)

He was the first person to win the 200m and 400m in the same Olympic game.

He was the first Black to win 4 Gold medals in the same Olympic game.

He was the first person (Black or White) to win the U. S. Amateur Golf Tournament, three years in a row.

He was the first Black Astronaut to travel into space.

He was the first Black person to win the U. S. Open Tennis Championship.

She was the first Black crowned "Miss America".

He was the first Black named Baseballs: "Rookie of the Year".

She was the first living trademark for a famous pancake mix.

She was the first Black schoolteacher and founder of the Phyllis Wheatley Home for Aged Black Women, in Detroit, Michigan.

He was the first Black to conduct a major symphony orchestra.

He was the first Black White House correspondent and received 19 Emmys for journalism.

He was the first Black man to cross the Alps.

He was named the first Black captain for the Yale University football team.

He became the first Black Heavyweight boxing champion.

He invented the first Cellular telephone.

He was the First Black to win both the 100m, 200m & 4 x 100m relays in the same Olympics, ALL with World records.

*All of the answers can be found in this book.

Copyright © Willie A. Price 2008

Historical Black Colleges (level 3)

ALABAMA (A&M)
ALCORN (STATE)
BENEDICT
BETHUNE COOKMAN
BLUEFIELD (STATE)
BOWIE (STATE)
CHARLES DREW
DILLARD
FLORIDA (A&M)
GRAMBLING
HAMPTON
HINDS (COMM. COLL.)
HOWARD
JACKSON (STATE)
LIVINGSTONE
MEHARRY (MEDICAL)
MOREHOUSE
MORGAN
MORRIS BROWN
NORFOLK (STATE)
PAINE
PRAIRIE VIEW
SELMA (UNIVERSITY)
SOUTHERN
SOUTHWESTERN
SPELMAN
ST PAULS
TRENHOLM
TUSKEGEE
VOORHEES
WILBERFORCE
WILEY (COLLEGE)
XAVIER

```
D L E I F E U L B W I L E Y K
G N I L B M A R G S T P A U L
B H P R A I R I E V I E W U O
B E N E D I C T A I N N S C F
N O T P M A H O W A R D H H R
A G R H R T E V P E O V I A O
L E E O U N U A T W C O N R N
A S N B M N I S Z B L O D L E
B U H S O N E Y K C A R S E C
A O O O E W R C X E A H Q S R
M H L U H R I A O L G E P D O
A E M T A D V E L O J E T R F
A R U H Z I Y I F K K S E E R
X O E E E L D L S E L M A W E
S M O R G A N S P E L M A N B
I M E N O T S G N I V I L N L
N W O R B S I R R O M B C V I
N O S K C A J F L O R I D A W
```

Copyright © Willie A. Price 2008

"Sounds Greek to Me" (Level 3)

Sounds "Greek" to me, is a salute to the original 8 Black Greek letter college organizations. How well do you know your Black Greek letter history? Can you tell which are the fraternities and which are the sororities? Where were the organization founded and what date was it founded? All of the answers can be found in this book.

Organization	Frat/Soror.	College Founded	Date Founded
Alpha Phi Alpha	_____	_____	_____
Alpha Kappa Alpha	_____	_____	_____
Zeta Phi Beta	_____	_____	_____
Phi Beta Sigma	_____	_____	_____
Kappa Alpha Psi	_____	_____	_____
Delta Sigma Theta	_____	_____	_____
Sigma Gamma Rho	_____	_____	_____
Omega Psi Phi	_____	_____	_____
Iota Phi Theta	_____	_____	_____

Copyright © Willie A. Price 2008

"Picture Me This"
Do you know these young men?

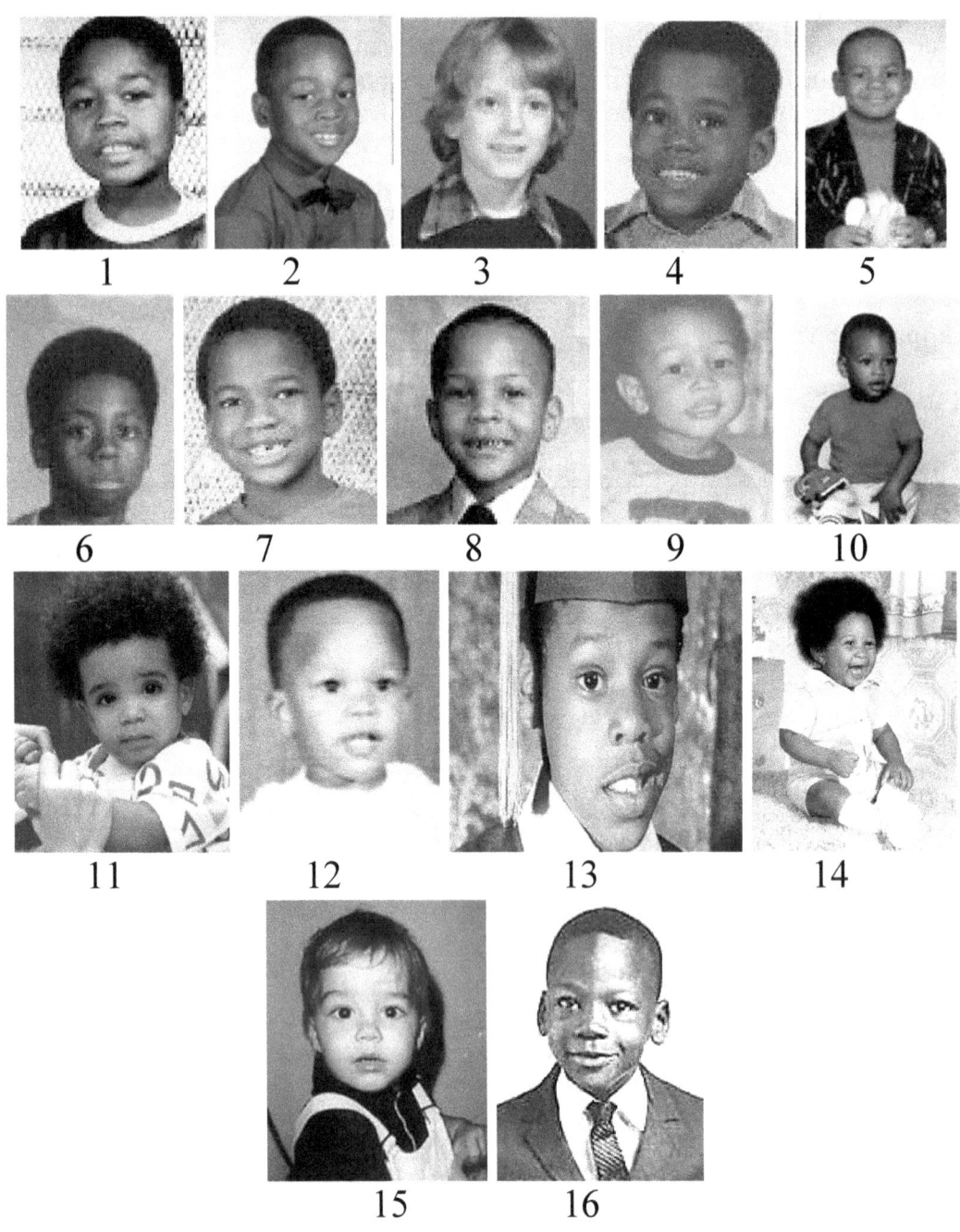

Copyright © Willie A. Price 2013

"Picture Me This"
Do you know these young Ladies?

Copyright © Willie A. Price 2013

WHAT'S MY NAME?

	Entertainment Name		Actual Name
1	JADAKISS	A	TAUHEED EPPS
2	BEANIE SIGEL	B	JOSEPH G. JONES
3	THE DREAM	C	TRAMAR DILLARD
4	GAME	D	ARMANDO C. PEREZ
5	2 CHAINZ	E	ONIKA T. MARAJ
6	JIM JONES	F	CAMERON THOMAZ
7	FLO RIDA	G	JAYSON PHILLIPS
8	PITBULL	H	TERIUS Y. NASH
9	NICKI MINAJ	I	DWIGHT GRANT
10	WIZ KHALIFA	J	JAYCEON T. TAYLOR

Copyright © Willie A. Price 2013

WHAT'S MY NAME?

	Entertainment Name		Actual Name
1	DRAKE	A	ROBERT R. WILLIAMS
2	SEAN KINGSTON	B	KARIM KHARBOUCH
3	SWIZZ BEATZ	C	KISEAN ANDERSON
4	LUPE FIASCO	D	GERMAINE WILLIAMS
5	CANIBUS	E	DeANDRE R. WAY
6	MEEK MILLS	F	WASALU M. JACO
7	WAKA FLOCKA FLAME	G	WILLIAM L. ROBERTS II
8	SOULJA BOY	H	JUAQUIN MALPHURS
9	FRENCH MONTANA	I	AUBREY GRAHAM
10	RICK ROSS	J	KASSEEM D. DEAN

Copyright © Willie A. Price 2013

WHAT'S MY NAME?

Entertainment Name	**Actual Name**
1 BILLIE HOLIDAY	A DANA OWENS
2 BIG SEAN	B NATALIE R. McINTYRE
3 JUELZ SANTANA	C THOMAS CALLAWAY
4 QUEEN LATIFAH	D ELEANOR FAGAN
5 BOBBY VALENTINO	E LARON JAMES
6 MACY GRAY	F S. MICHAEL ANDERSON
7 BONE CRUSHER	G JAY JENKINS
8 YOUNG JEEZY	H ROBERT WILSON
9 CEELO	I WAYNE HARDNETT

Copyright © Willie A. Price 2013

"Ladies of Soul"

AMERIE	A	B	E	R	Y	K	A	H	B	A	D	U
ANGIE STONE	C	S	W	D	S	E	H	F	I	G	J	P
ARETHA FRANKLIN	N	C	H	A	K	A	K	H	A	N	K	A
ASHANTI	I	H	I	A	L	M	D	N	P	O	E	T
CHAKA KHAN	L	A	T	Q	N	R	T	E	S	U	I	T
CHRISETTE MICHELLE	K	F	N	V	A	T	W	B	X	C	R	I
ERYKAH BADU	N	I	E	Y	E	Z	I	F	G	D	A	L
EVE	A	T	Y	H	T	A	M	I	A	N	M	A
INDIA ARIE	R	A	H	A	L	I	C	J	G	E	A	B
<u>MISSY</u> ELLIOT	F	L	O	K	B	H	D	I	I	E	N	E
PATTI LaBELLE	A	N	U	F	P	G	E	R	O	S	I	L
QUEEN LATIFAH	H	E	S	I	M	S	A	N	E	D	T	L
SADE	T	E	T	Q	T	A	M	I	A	R	B	E
TAMIA	E	U	O	O	I	U	R	I	O	D	A	C
TINA MARIE	R	Q	N	D	R	E	E	U	S	T	X	H
TINA TURNER	A	E	N	K	M	C	J	V	I	S	G	E
WHITNEY HOUSTON	T	I	N	A	T	U	R	N	E	R	Y	Q

Copyright Willie A. Price 2013

"Sisters of R and B"

ALICIA KEYS	O	L	I	V	I	A	B	C	A	D	G
BEYONCE	D	A	E	B	E	Y	O	N	C	E	H
BLU CANTRELL	H	D	L	T	L	C	Y	B	I	U	A
BRANDY	L	Z	E	I	O	M	Q	N	N	O	K
CHRISETTE MICHELLE	A	B	H	D	C	E	R	H	O	J	E
CIARA	S	V	C	V	A	I	M	Q	M	K	R
JORDAN SPARKS	K	A	I	C	I	G	A	J	K	E	I
KELLY ROWLAND	R	B	M	Q	H	J	R	K	L	L	H
KERI HILSON	A	N	E	R	S	D	Y	U	E	L	I
KEYSHIA COLE	P	W	T	D	Y	B	J	H	Y	Y	L
MARY J. BLIGE	S	E	T	A	E	R	B	N	M	R	S
MONICA	N	M	E	N	K	L	L	Z	X	O	O
OLIVIA	A	Q	S	N	M	A	I	S	D	W	N
RIHANNA	D	C	I	A	R	A	G	F	G	L	H
	R	W	R	H	J	X	E	C	V	A	B
	O	E	H	I	O	P	A	S	D	N	F
	J	R	C	R	T	Y	U	I	O	D	P
	B	L	U	C	A	N	T	R	E	L	L

Copyright Willie A. Price 2013

Answer Page

WHAT'S MY NAME?	RIDDLE ME THIS?	WHAT'S MY NAME?
Page 81	**Page 82**	**Page 84**
1 H	1 BROWN	A 14
2 M	2 MOSES	B 17
3 L	3 PEANUT	C 19
4 O	4 SMITH	D 13
5 I	5 WILLIAMS	E 1
6 P	6 KING	F 7
7 F	7 WASHINGTON	G 18
8 C	8 WRITER	H 10
9 A	9 CREAM	I 6
10 B	10 FRAME	J 3
11 N	11 PAPER	K 2
12 J	12 PAN	L 15
13 E	13 SHOE	M 5
14 G	14 JACKSON	N 8
	15 ALAN	O 11
	16 WEST	P 20
	17 WAYNE	Q 12
		R 16
		S 4
		T 9

*NOTE: The purpose of this book is to get the reader involved in reading and researching the information. If the game states that the answers are in the book. The reader is encouraged to locate the answers within the pages of the book or on the internet.

Answer Page

88 PICTURE ME THIS?
1. 50 CENT
2. DWAYNE WADE
3. EMINEM
4. KANYE WEST
5. LaBRON JAMES
6. LiL WAYNE
7. NEYO
8. T.I.
9. JOHN LEGEND
10. TREY SONGZ
11. DRAKE
12. JAMIE FOXX
13. JAY Z
14. USHER
15. RICKY MARTIN
16. MICHAEL JORDAN

89 PICTURE ME THIS?
1. JENNIFER LOPEZ
2. KIM KARDASHIAN
3. MARIAH CAREY
4. ALICIA KEYS
5. ASHANTI
6. CIARA
7. QUEEN LaTIFAH
8. RIHANNA
9. TINA TURNER
10. BEYONCE
11. HALLE BERRY
12. JANET JACKSON

Answer Page

WHAT'S MY NAME?
PAGE: 90
1 G
2 I
3 H
4 J
5 A
6 B
7 C
8 D
9 E
10 F

WHAT'S MY NAME?
PAGE: 91
1 I
2 C
3 J
4 F
5 D
6 A
7 H
8 E
9 B
10 G

WHAT'S MY NAME?
PAGE: 92
1 D
2 F
3 E
4 A
5 H
6 B
7 I
8 G
9 C

Black Inventors and The areas of their Inventions

A.P. ABOURNE	REFINING OF COCONUT OIL
AFRICANS	PAPER
AFRICANS	CHESS
AFRICANS	MEDICINE
AFRICANS	CIVILIZATION
AFRICANS	ALPHABET
JAMES ADAMS	AEROPLANE PROPELLING DEVICE
L.C. BAILEY	FOLDING BED
BENJAMIN BANNEKER	BLUE PRINTS FOR WASHINGTON, D.C.
BENJAMIN BANNEKER	1ST ALMANAC, CLOCK
JAMES BAUER	COIN CHANGER
ANDREW BEARD	ROTARY ENGINE
ANDREW BEARD	TRAIN CAR COUPLER
G.E. BECKET	LETTER BOX (MAILBOX)
HENRY BLAIR	CORN PLANTER
HENRY BLAIR	COTTON PLANTER
SARAH BOONE	IRONING BOARD
OTIS BOYKIN	PACE MAKER CONTROL
OTIS BOYKIN	GUIDED MISSILE
CHARLES BROOKS	STREET SWEEPER
PHIL BROOKS	DISPOSABLE SYRINGE
MARIE BROWN	HOME SECURITY SYSTEM
JOHN A. BURR	LAWN MOWER
BURRIDGE & MARCHMAN	TYPEWRITER

GEORGE CARRUTHERS	RADIATION DETECTOR
GEORGE W. CARVER	PEANUT BUTTER
GEO. W CARVER	PAINTS & STAINS
GEO. W. CARVER	LOTIONS & SOAP
GEORGE COOK	AUTOMATIC FISHING REEL
ALFRED L CRALLE	ICE CREAM SCOOPER
G. DOWNING & W. DESJARDIN	CORNER CLEANER ATTACHMENT
JOSEPH DICKINSON	ARM FOR RECORD PLAYER
O. DORSEY	DOOR STOP
O. DORSEY	DOOR KNOB
P. B. DOWNING	POSTAL LETTER BOX
PHILLIP DOWNING	WORLD FASTEST COMPUTER
DR. CHARLES DREW	BLOOD PLASMA
T. ELKINS	TOILET
ROBERT FLEMING Jr.	GUITAR
GEORGE F. GRANT	GOLF TEE
MICHAEL HARNEY	LANTERN
WM. HARWELL	SPACE SHUTTLE RETRIEVAL ARM
LYDIA HOLMES	WOOD TOYS PATENT
AUGUSTUS JACKSON	ICE CREAM
H. A. JACKSON	KITCHEN TABLE
JOSEPH N. JACKSON	PROGRAMABLE REMOTE CONTROL
JOSEPH N. JACKSON	VIDEO COMMANDER
ISSAC R. JOHNSON	BICYCLE FRAME
JOHN A. JOHNSON	WRENCH
LONNIE JOHNSON	SUPER SOAKER WATER GUN

W. JOHNSON	EGG BEATER
FREDERICK M. JONES	REFRIGERATION DEFROSTER
FREDERICK M. JONES	AIR CONDITIONING UNIT
FREDERICK M. JONES	TWO-CYCLE GAS ENGINE
FREDERICK M. JONES	INTERNAL COMBUSTION ENGINE
FREDERICK M. JONES	STARTER GENERATOR
FREDERICK M. JONES	REFRIGERATION CONTROLS
LATIMER & NICHOLS	ELECTRIC LAMP
W. A. LAVALETTE	PRINTING PRESS
MAURICE W. LEE	PRESSURE COOKER
A. L. LEWIS	WINDOW CLEANER
JOHN L. LOVE	PENCIL SHARPENER
TOM MARSHALL	FIRE EXTINGUISHER
W. A. MARTIN	LOCK
ALEXANDER MILES	ELEVATOR
GARRETT MORGAN	GAS MASK
GARRETT MORGAN	TRAFFIC SIGNAL
LYDA NEWMAN	HAIR BRUSH
ALICE H. PARKER	HEATING FURNACE
J. F. PICKERING	AIRSHIP (BLIMP)
PURDY / SADGWAR	FOLDING CHAIR
HENRY SAMPSON	CELLULAR TELEPHONE
W. B. PURVIS	FOUTAIN PIN
L. P. RAY	DUST PAN
W. H. RICHARDSON	BABY BUGGY

WALTER SAMMONS	PRESSING COMB
G. T. SAMPSON	CLOTHES DRIER
DEWEY SANDERSON	URINALYSIS MACHINE
RALPH SANDERSON	HYDRAULIC SHOCK ABSORBER
S. R. SCOTTRON	CURTAIN ROD
J. W. SMITH	LAWN SPRINKLER
FOLARIN SOSAN	PACKAGE-PARK
J. STANDARD	REFRIGERATOR
T. W. STEWART	MOP
MADAME C.J. WALKER	COSMETICS & HAIR CARE PRODUCTS
MANLEY WEST	CANIBIS CURE FOR GLAUCOMA
PAUL E. WILLIAMS	HELICOPTER
J. B. WINTERS	FIRE ESCAPE LADDER
GRANVILLE T. WOODS	TELEPHONE SYSTEM
GRANVILLE T. WOODS	ELECTRIC RAILWAY SYSTEM
GRANVILLE T. WOODS	ROLLER COASTER

New Inventions & Inventors

Notes

References

The Black Chronicle Magazine, by Maloyd Ben Wilson: A compilation of newspaper articles dating from 1776 – 1956. Documenting the

"This Week in Black History": Monthly articles by W. A. Price
January, February, March, April, May, June, July, August, September, October, November, December.

TheBlackMarket.com (Black History Calendars): Verification and follow-up to information in the book. 2006, 2007

The Challenger News Paper, Buffalo, N.Y.: "This Week in Black History" Self-published articles. Additional information acquired from other weekly publications of the newspaper. 2000 – 2008 articles.

The Think Quest New York City 2007 articles

AOL.Com News Center: News articles and research sources: 2006, 2007, 2008 articles.

WIKIPEDIA.COM:
Various Biography articles: 2006, 2007, 2008, 2009, 2010, 2011, 2012.

Gabrielle Douglas Official Website: Photos and Biography.

Tia Norfleet Official Website: Photos and Biography.

Photographs

WIKIPEDIA.COM: Various Biography articles 2008, 2013

Biggeststars.com: 2008, Jesseowens.com: 2008

Image Printers, Monwell Floyd, Willie A. Price

KINGS OF AFRICA are Photographs by Daniel LAINÉ: 2006

Ernestine Shepherd: Doll houseHealthyHair.com, Donloree.com, Dbtechno.com, Nhatrang Club, Stek.org, Dykai.eu, Muscleiuhu.org, Forumbodybuilding.com, Addmorejuice.com

Barack Obama & Family: abcnews.com, binsidetv.net, brainz.org, dailymail.co.uk, dosomething.org, Igbofocus.com, mpetrelis.blogspot.com, obamadiary.org, roc4life.com, usatoday.com

Order Form

The Black Chronicle Magazine   This Week in Black History

Black History Game Book

MAIL PAYMENT TO:
Willie A. Price Speaks
P. O. BOX 603
BUFFALO, NY 14215

* For speaking engagements use the contact information below.

E-MAIL: WillieAPrice@aol.com
www.WillieAPriceSpeaks.com

*ALLOW 5-7 DAYS AFTER PAYMENT RECEIVED FOR SHIPMENT FROM N.Y. STATE.

Name: _____ (Print)

Address: _____

City: _____ State: _____ Zip: _____

Telephone: (___) _____

E-Mail: _____

The Black Chronicles: _____ X $20.00 = $_____

This Week in Black History: _____ X $20.00 = $_____

(S & H: U.S.A.) # of books: _____ X $ 5.00 = $_____

Total Amount Enclosed: $_____

Payment:

Certified Check ( ) Money Order ( ) **(No cash/personal checks)**

* Request information about our fundraiser book sale program or discounted bulk orders.

www.ingramcontent.com/pod-product-compliance
Lightning Source LLC
Chambersburg PA
CBHW080406170426
43193CB00016B/2826